T0163972

extraordinary journey—from surface to depth, from exterior to interior, a spiritual odyssey that is truly of our time, genuine in its care, redeeming in its grace." —Ken Wilbur, author of *A Brief History of Everything*

"Can a man who has been put through the wringer by life...actually write a memoir free of self-pity? Mark Matousek has done it. Even more remarkably, he has written a book about (spiritual) fulfillment without once sounding flaky....you'll find it hard not to admire a man so determined to find a deeper meaning in a difficult life....Prose that sings....Matousek comes to a realization of life's wonders in a scene that will leave no reader unmoved." —*People Magazine*

"With the speed and brilliance of a meteor....it is bound to elicit comparisons with Robert Pirsig's amazing 1974 memoir, *Zen and the Art of Motorcycle Maintenance*, for its narrative of a man seeking his place in the world by attempting to synthesize Western culture and Eastern spirituality.....Almost compulsively readable. His perseverance...and the truce wrested from his struggle—much like the story of Jacob wrestling with the angel—will inspire many readers." —*Echo Magazine*

"This is a candid and courageous account of one man's search for spiritual meaning—an inspiring book, full of hope." —Andrew T. Weil, M.D., author of *Spontaneous Healing*

"This strangely compelling book opens and opens into unexpected depths. *Sex Death Enlightenment* is the story of a bold, skeptical, down-to-earth soul willing to be educated by the hardest things in the world, willing to look into the face of despair and death and come up from that black and bitter embrace changed, open-hearted, eager to live." —Mark Doty, author of *Heaven's Gate*

SEX
DEATH
ENLIGHTENMENT

A TRUE STORY

MARK MATOUSEK

MONKFISH BOOK PUBLISHING COMPANY
RHINEBECK, NEW YORK

Paperback ISBN 978-1-948626-25-5
eBook ISBN 978-1-948626-26-2

Library of Congress Control Number: 2020943155

Cover design by Lisa Carta
Book design by Colin Rolfe

Monkfish Book Publishing Company
22 East Market Street
Suite 304
Rhinebeck, NY 12572
(845) 876-4861
monkfishpublishing.com

For Carole Snyder
Beloved friend and sister

Dark enemy, you who brace us in the fight
Let me, in the few days left to spend
Devote my strength and weakness to the light
And so be changed to lightning in the end.
—Marina Tsvetayeva

CONTENTS

PREFACE

THERE ARE FEW things more disconcerting for a writer than meeting the ghost of your much younger self in the pages of a decades-old memoir. You feel a smorgasbord of emotions watching this character as he wrestles with the drama of his existence: embarrassment, empathy, horror, affection, gratitude, disbelief, pleasure, regret. It's like running into a distant relation who looks like you, never gets old, and tells the same story again and again.

When *Sex Death Enlightenment* was published in June 1996, I believed it would be my last book. I was infected with a fatal virus and thought I'd be dead within a few years, which gave me very little time—and one shot only—to communicate the story I wanted to tell, about a selfish, cynical, New York social and professional climber confronting his own mortality, going on a spiritual adventure, and returning home a different man. The word *catastrophe* comes from the Greek for "to turn around," which is exactly what disaster did for me: stopped me in my arrogant tracks, forced me to face my buried pain, and thrust me into exploring questions I'd done my best to ignore until then. Who was this person I called myself? Why did I feel like such an impostor? What was this longing at the pit of my stomach for something I had no words for, this hunger for mystery, truth, and connection that began in childhood and then became buried under ambition, greed, and anxiety? Was there a purpose to life,

I needed to know, and what about a divine Creator? Did such an intelligent force exist, or was this nothing more than a fantasy of the collective human imagination in need of a comforting opiate fix?

These were the questions I pursued in extremis, and because I'd found some intriguing answers and had mysterious experiences I could not deny, I wanted to write a book for hard-headed, skeptical people like myself who don't believe in fairy tales but are inquisitive enough to keep an open mind. When this journey begins, my character is an insecure egomaniac convinced that his flat-Earth view of things is more or less accurate. By Chapter Five, he's shocked into seeing he knows almost nothing, that miracles happen, and that life does, indeed, have a purpose: to awaken to mysteries beyond comprehension, including his own essential nature. In order for this to happen, though, he'll need to tell the whole truth as he knows it and face himself without turning away.

I wanted to write a spiritual book for worldly people—a doubt-filled, genre-busting, hybrid memoir that combined sacred and profane, holy and irreverent, sublime and ridiculous, as they're mixed together in real life. But how to describe metaphysical insight without sounding fatuous, flaky, or fake? Having returned from India with my mind blown to pieces, with a convert's zeal to spread the good news, I'd made a fool of myself on several occasions— attempting to describe what happened to me in esoteric, pretentious language— and I knew that approach would fail on the page. My challenge was to describe what had happened, including the otherworldly parts, as plainly and truthfully as possible, in hopes that readers dubious of such experiences might feel intrigued enough to take their own journey beyond the limits of their rational minds.

I threw myself into writing in a basement room on Charles Street in the West Village of New York City, in June 1994. I arrived before seven o'clock every morning and pounded away on my old Selectric until my eyes were falling out of my head and my legs were cramped from not moving for hours. I was working on a ridiculous publishing deadline (fourteen months to deliver a completed manuscript), but more than that, my health clock was ticking louder by the day. I had no clue how to write a memoir, so I made a list of what seemed to be essential moments for telling the story and committed to drafting a scene a day—which, like my deadline, was absurd. The list was twice as long as it needed to be (who knew?) and I tore through it, scene after scene, day after day, Monday through Saturday for a year. I covered the walls of the dreary little room with pinned-up piles of color-coded paper, cut into various configurations, covered with rows of messy single-spaced type, until the room resembled the inside of a frantic brain turned inside out.

By the end of that year, I'd written over seven hundred pages, and when I finished (what I thought would be) the end, I gathered the pages into a two-foot-high pile and carried the manuscript, like a mother swaddling a baby, out of the basement and into the street, cradling it in my arms. I remember the warmth of the sun on my face and feeling delirious, ravaged, like I'd come through a monumental labor, but was happier than ever before in my life.

After this came the baby's vivisection, which I was unable to face alone. Barbara, my dear friend and an excellent, Samurai editor, agreed to take a month off to guide the surgery. The two of us sat on the floor of my apartment, surrounded by paper on all sides, as Barbara sliced through the mass of excess fat and I looked on in despair and excitement. After four weeks, the manuscript had been whittled down by half and I was happy, more or less (the truth is, a book can always be better). When I delivered it to my editor, she read it immediately, seemed blown away, and proceeded to give me the kind of publishing experience every first-time author dreams about: book tours, interviews, critical attention. My association with Andy Warhol opened a lot of doors with gossip-seeking mainstream journalists who came away disappointed to hear that Andy was just my boss, and not a person I liked to hang out with. Those same reporters dismissed the spirituality in the book as the magical thinking of a dead man walking, while spiritual publications embraced *Sex Death Enlightenment* immediately. What amazed me most was the appeal this story had for readers wildly different from me, and from every imaginable walk of life. Secretly, I'd worried that my story was too extreme, peculiar, mystical, or gay to cross the divide into mainstream culture or touch people living "normal" lives. In fact, the opposite proved to be true. My wise friend Florence predicted this when I came to her in a fit of worry that memoir-writing seemed so narcissistic and self-absorbed. That's when Florence set me straight: "When people are reading about you, they're not reading about you. They're reading about themselves." I realized she was right. My only job was to tell the truth, pull no punches, and trust that folks would find what they needed in what I had to say—or not.

That's what I tell my writing students: be as shameless, brave, and unfettered as possible, especially in the first draft; use the page as a sacred offering of what it means to be fully human; hold nothing back, fear no one, remember you can burn it later; pour your heart and originality into this work, and trust the inspiration—the initial impulse—that made you want to write this thing in the first place. Have the courage to meet your life, especially the mysterious parts, with openness, discernment, and wonder. Don't waste the chance to know yourself, pursue the questions that really matter, or forget how much there is to learn, still, regardless of how old you are. Remember that life comes and goes in a second and nothing lasts—or increases—but wisdom.

I'm grateful every day that I'm still here, and I'm intensely aware of how lucky I've been while so many others have died around me. Aristotle described good luck as the moment on the battlefield when the arrow hits the guy next to you. It's an awesome, miraculous, torn-in-half feeling—partly shattering, partly sublime. *Awe* is the only word that approaches describing it.

Trust your voice. It's all you've got. Trust your path because it's your life. I hope this book is a friend to you.

Mark Matousek
Springs, New York
March 22, 2020

PART ONE
TELL ME YOU LOVE ME, ANDY WARHOL

ONE

I T'S HARD TO know when you're having a breakdown in New York City. The symptoms of living here, succeeding here, and losing your mind here are almost identical.

At 9:30 P.M. on the night of my twenty-eighth birthday, I was sitting at my desk at *Interview* magazine, working furiously on the transcript of a question-and-answer session between Nancy Reagan and a Washington socialite—slashing, twisting, and coloring pages with red pencil—doing everything short of fabrication to make the first lady sound intelligent on paper. We were three days behind on our monthly deadline, and outside my office the staff was in hysterics: proofreaders running up and down the stairs with storyboards; paste-up girls snarling at their tables, wielding X-Acto knives; fashion assistants slamming racks of couture down the hall; the art director throwing together last-minute photo layouts of prone men in leather masks with weights strapped to their scrotums. Doris, the boss, was on the phone, loudly telling a writer to go fuck himself, while Sheila, the four-hundred-pound circulation director, nodded emphatic support and Glenn, the managing editor, ran back and forth, trying to hold the whole ridiculous mess together.

I was holed up alone as usual, toilet paper stuffed in my ears, bone tired from another seventy-hour workweek, unscrambling syntax and waiting to get the hell out of this place.

*

I couldn't see my breakdown coming, for three obvious reasons: First, I'd always been a little crazy, not *clinically*, just over-intense, compulsive, prone to a variety of erotic addictions and narcissistic mood swings—euphoria to despair in three seconds flat. Second, the backdrop of my breakdown—New York in the eighties—was insane in itself. Third, and most important, I was plugged into the epicenter of that insanity, working for Andy Warhol, the grand vizier of meaninglessness and the most famous artist in the world.

In the three years since I had started working at *Interview*, Andy had come to symbolize everything that was wrong with the world: hype and cleverness without soul, a Technicolor surface without depth, a glittering facade fashioned from fame, name, and money. It was an inverted zone, where everything and everyone is reduced to an object and put on sale, where everyone has his fifteen minutes—I starfuck, therefore I am—where the serious is BORING, the fluffy FABULOUS, and behind the great mask of glamour and image, nothing but an abyss.

It wasn't always like this. For a long time, this world thrilled me. With every hoop my bosses held up, I jumped higher. Nothing could stop me. I was *making it*, living my dream, proving that I could cut it in the toughest city on earth. New York was the big game, and I adored it.

I'd first fallen in love with the city ten years before, at fifteen, when my girlfriend, Tammi, and I ran away from Los Angeles to tap-dance our way onto Broadway. I'd just gotten out of jail for the second time that year after an incident involving a handful of Quaaludes, two demolished parked cars, and an attempt to beat up the policeman who found me with my head smashed through the windshield. I remember only flashes of the rough scene that followed: the cops cuffing my hands to the back of the chair and kicking it over backward; the look on my mother's face when she came to bail me out and saw me barefoot in overalls, my face caked with blood, bleached hair sticking out like Rasta doo-doo braids. As we left the building, Ida turned to me and said, "You're gonna end up in Alcatraz."

She was right. I *was* headed for a life in prison if I didn't move fast. I was going stir crazy in suburbia, raging and desperate to break out. For most of that year, I sat in my bedroom like a prisoner, smoking joints and covering the walls from floor to ceiling with crazy poems and obscenities.

My nympho girlfriend, Tammi, saved me. One day, after we'd done it in the backseat of my mother's car, she rolled over and said she had a surprise for me: a friend in Brooklyn had offered to put us up. The next day I cashed in my $500 bar mitzvah bond and bought two one-way tickets to Kennedy airport. My Russian grandfather, who'd worked in a button factory to bring his family from the Bronx to the promised land of the San Fernando Valley, threatened to disown me. My mother, in a final, halfhearted attempt to take control of her criminal son, swore to have the police waiting for us at the other end. I packed my bags, kissed her goodbye and left, knowing she'd never make good on her threat.

I'll never forget coming up out of the West Side subway on Christopher Street for the first time. Surfacing across from the Stonewall Bar, staring at Sheridan Square swarming with tourists, street kids, queers of every shape and size, I knew that I had found my home. I'd finally found a place that was as loud, bright, fractured, and intense as I felt inside. Wearing one of Tammi's Bowie-inspired ensembles—plaid pants and jacket, fake fur collar, and green platform shoes—I stood there watching this wonderful circus pass by. New York matched my idea of how huge and outrageous my life could be. Its scale was *my* scale. I could fit in here and start all over, three thousand miles away from my mother, those old memories, all that bad blood.

We lasted a week. One night, at a bar on Tenth Street called the Ninth Circle, Tammi and I were carrying an overdosing junkie out onto the sidewalk when a cop car passed by. We dropped him on the pavement and ran all the way to the Hudson River, terrified that we'd be arrested for murder. We hid in a phone booth and called my mother, begging for money to come home. When our plane took off the next day, I looked down at the skyscrapers and swore to come back as soon as I could.

Ten years later, having been rehabilitated by my lover, Bob (who convinced me I was wasting my life and sent me off to college in Berkeley), I moved east with a master's in English lit and hopes of becoming a writer. Desperate to get my name into print, I took any reporting job I could get. I reviewed off-Broadway plays for a throwaway rag. I did wire stories for Reuters at $75 apiece, laboring endlessly over my deathless prose (which they ripped to shreds) and distinguishing myself as the last journalist to talk to the producer of *Oh! Calcutta!* before he jumped out the window of the Edison Hotel. I spent the summer as an intern editor in the letters department of *Newsweek* magazine, patronizing angry readers, and was eventually fired for not being what my tight-assed boss called a company man.

After six months in New York, I was starting to worry that I'd never get a permanent job when a friend of a friend who taught aerobics to the editor of *Interview* offered to get me in the door. As I walked across Union Square toward Andy Warhol's Factory that autumn afternoon, in my penny loafers and three-piece corduroy suit, I thought, this is *it*, my big break about to happen.

Everyone had heard of Andy Warhol. He was the albino soup-can man, the man who turned a camera on the Empire State Building for a day and called it art, who gave us teen porn star Joe Dallesandro buck naked on the big screen, who surrounded himself with stoned-out superstars and drag queens—Viva, Candy Darling, Edie Sedgwick— the director who made an entire theater crowd gag during a screening of *Frankenstein* by dangling a dripping human liver in 3-D over their congregated heads. This was the Andy Warhol I was about to meet, and I was determined to make him love me.

When I stepped off the elevator at the Factory, I was mobbed by pug dogs. The puffy blonde receptionist smoking a cigarette took one look at me and went back to her magazine. I stood there and stared at the amazing loft, the huge Technicolor portraits, messy cubbyholes, antiques, taxidermy, piles of junk. Cute boys in tight jeans bustled here and there. Still, the receptionist did not acknowledge my presence. Trying to appear at ease, I knelt to pet the dogs. That got her attention. "Don't touch them!" she snapped. "Who are you?"

I told her I was there to see Robert Hayes, the editor. She directed me to a cubicle where a slight, balding man wearing a muffler was hunched over a contact sheet with a magnifying glass. The walls were plastered with glamour shots of Liza's eyelashes, Halston in his turtleneck, and still lifes by Robert Mapplethorpe—calla lilies and enormous black penises.

"You're Dick's friend?" he said, looking up at me staring at the photos.

I nodded and handed him my clips and résumé. He gave them a quick once-over and handed them back to me.

"You're a writer?"

"I want to be."

"Then this is not the place for you. Nobody writes here. Nobody even reads." Hayes saw I was confused. "We illustrate pictures. No one gives a fuck about words. Least of all Andy."

"Really?"

"He's never read a book in his life. Except his bankbook. He asked me once why I couldn't make the magazine nothing but ads, just pages of splashy ads with gorgeous models and dollar signs. Isn't that literary? Doesn't that bathe you in inspiration?"

"Not really."

"What about lunch with The Bangles? Or spending two hours on the phone with someone's publicist because she didn't like her hair on the cover? Would that be your idea of art?"

"Not really, but I've got to work."

"Then wait tables. Turn tricks. Do anything, but *don't* be a patsy. I wanted to be an artist once. That's why I came to the city—to be an art photographer, Cartier-Bresson. Then I met Andy and got swept up in all this shit."

"But people would kill for your job."

"They've tried, honey, but, trust me, nothing here is what it appears to be. Least of all *him*," he said, pointing to a shot of Andy holding a camera in front of his face. "The great pretender, now you see him, now you don't." As he said this, Robert Hayes was seized by a coughing fit, and I noticed for the first time how unwell he looked, sallow and terribly thin.

"Sorry," he said, collecting himself. "The point is, I spend my time underpaying other photographers to do work I should be doing myself. If you care about being an artist, stop trying to be a success. It's the kiss of death." Hayes took a handkerchief from his pocket and dabbed at his forehead. "Is it hot in here?" he asked.

"No," I said. In fact, the office was chilly.

"Must be the change. I'll be the youngest queen in New York to go through menopause. Maybe I'll finally get a square jaw." Hayes stood up to indicate that our meeting was over.

As I turned to go, a zaftig brunette in a velvet headband passed by carrying a large piece of cardboard. "Here's Dr. Mengele," whispered Hayes. "Doris, come meet someone."

"I'm busy."

"He's cute."

The woman stepped back. "Hi, how are *you*?" she asked in a nasal monotone, shaking an enormous diamond wedding ring in my direction. "Are you a friend of Andy's?"

"No, I'm looking for a job. Do you know of anything?"

"Good-*bye*, Mark," said Hayes.

"Can you please help me?" I asked.

Doris looked at me. "Can you spell?"

"I'm a *writer*."

"He's overqualified," said Hayes.

"I'll bet he is," said Doris, staring at my crotch. "Look, we're on deadline. I need someone to proof the boards."

"I could do that."

"All right," said Doris, shooting a superior look at Hayes. "Come meet Andy."

She led me around a corner to a dark, cavernous room that resembled the backstage of a theater. There, in the middle of a colossal mess of canvases, lumber, and garbage, sat Andy Warhol—a pale wisp in a fright wig, black turtleneck, and black jeans—working with a preppie male assistant. On the wall was a five-by-five projection of the jowly crowned face of a dictator's wife, overlaid with colored paint.

Andy was pointing at the photograph and telling the young man which colors to fill in.

"He's doing a portrait commission. Isn't it *greeaat*?" Doris whispered.

"Really great," I said.

"He's a genius."

"Yes."

We stood for several minutes watching the genius point at the contours of his subject's face, like a child with a coloring book, until the chubby cheeks were decoratively shaded with magenta, yellow, and aquamarine. Finally Andy told the assistant to freeze what they'd done.

Feeling like Dorothy in *The Wizard of Oz*, I approached and Doris introduced me. Andy turned his pale face toward me and stared without blinking through his pink glasses. It was the scariest (living) face I'd ever seen, shiny, plasticized skin, the eyes blank and shallow. "I'm really glad to meet you," I said, my stomach dropping as he stared.

Warhol lifted his hand in slow motion. When I took the limp thing, it was strangely mushy—like boiled chicken—and felt as if the skin would come sliding off the bone if I pulled too hard. "*Greeaat*," he drawled for no apparent reason.

"Fantastic place you have here," I said.

Andy's eyes shot to Doris, who said, "Okay, that's it."

"*Greeaat*," Andy drawled again, turning back to the projection on the wall.

Luckily, I didn't have to deal with him much. He hovered in the background, filtering his complaints through Doris, who worked us to the bone for pennies. I didn't care. I had a job, and though it was menial, being attached to Andy's name, working in the famous Factory, gave it more cachet than the "legit" jobs my friends had in publishing. Movie stars, rock singers, millionaires, Nobel laureates, politicians, porn stars, famous wives, children, and mistresses streamed in and out of the office every day; and though I was far too vain to be starstruck, bumping into Grace Jones coming out of the can did give me the sense that I was becoming famous too. I threw myself into the magazine, determined to become indispensable and to climb the masthead from drone to editor.

Interview, which Andy had founded in the sixties as a showcase for his famous friends, had as its gimmick the tape-recorded Q&A interview. These were not your slick *Rolling Stone* kind of conversations but—in keeping with Andy's aesthetic of raising the most banal to the level of art (or, at least, public record)—verbatim transcriptions of every fart and whisper that happened during encounters between the people that Andy wanted to showcase. The names that made it into *Interview* fell into seven distinct classes: young, beautiful, rich, famous, groupies, scandalmongers, and advertisers. Andy had an uncanny knack for mixing and matching these groups in print, creating his own surreal mix of brilliance and worthlessness, deconstructing both in the process. Hence, the Nobel laureate would be questioned by the heroin addict at the Chelsea Hotel; the Oscar winner would meet the has-been socialite for a shopping spree at Barneys. Whenever possible, we cross-pollinated the ultrafamous with the ultrafamous over cannoli at Elaine's—with a third party (frequently me) there to work the recorder and pay the bill. These meetings were sometimes fun and sometimes dull, but it didn't matter as long as there was *dirt*. Decades before Robin Leach exploited the lifestyles of the rich and famous, Andy was publishing his unadorned insta-takes of clashing titans and mindless tramps, creating a niche for *Interview* in the halls of pop journalism.

Luckily for me, few of the magazine's contributors could write worth a damn, which gave me an edge. I soon mastered the art of the zippy phrase and became known at the magazine as the Blurb King, sticking in adjectives like plastic surgeon's pins, nipping and tucking, applying generous gobs of bullshit to make anybody, and everybody, look GREEAAT. I spent my days ghostwriting hundreds of introductions and articles, signing famous names instead of mine, mastering the reporter's trick of writing with apparent authority about things I knew absolutely nothing about.

In two years I was promoted from part-time proofreader to staff writer to senior editor. After that, whenever I bumped into Andy outside the locked bathroom where he reportedly stashed his wigs, he nodded at me instead of pretending I didn't exist. When Robert Hayes, whose health had been in decline since my arrival at the magazine, was hospitalized with the pneumonia that would eventually kill him, Doris gave me his office. And though I felt guilty emptying his drawers into cardboard boxes while he was lying in a bed at Lenox Hill Hospital, I was equally thrilled by the highly visible promotion.

Every so often, however, when I made the mistake of taking a serious look at what I was actually doing, I did my best to shut myself up, convincing myself that mine were privileged problems. How could I complain about lunches with movie stars, film screenings, free tickets, invitations to parties, constant solicitations from publicists who treated me like a VIP? Though I was perfectly aware of how tinny all this was beneath the perks, I whitewashed my conscience with the excuse that I was just biding my time till something better came along, paying my dues till my next break. When the sheer absurdity of having to sing the praises of Calvin Klein's latest poster boy made me doubt my own credibility, I comforted myself with the thought that this was just my first stop on a more significant journey, that my real life hadn't started yet and I'd be out of there at the first opportunity.

It's hard to say exactly when my breakdown started, but sometime in the winter of 1985, everything began to fall apart emotionally. I began having panic attacks—daylong bouts of depression under my bedcovers with the phone machine turned off. I tried to write off this growing anxiety to stress—the grind of the year-in, year-out climbing, straining to hold my own in the midst of chaos. But the distress I felt was more mysterious than that, and had less to do with my career than with an inner loss of meaning. Though I now had had nearly everything I'd always wanted, I'd become increasingly aware as that winter wore on of a nagging, growing yearning inside me, a hunger I could not seem to satisfy. The higher I climbed on the masthead, the more successful my life appeared on the outside, the more secretly dishonest I felt. At times this hunger felt like a knot in my solar plexus, a rock-hard fist of grief clenched so tight at times that I couldn't breathe. In those weeks and months before I realized what was happening, this fist would choke me at unexpected moments— during meetings, interviews, dinners with friends—sometimes sending me into the bathroom, panting like a dog, struggling to catch my breath. When this suffocation overcame me I was flooded with a strange emotion—or something deeper than emotion, a kind of growing soul sickness. I could almost hear the steady, moaning noise in my gut at these times, like someone starving and crying out for help. I didn't understand this voice or what it was asking for; I knew only that more and more, at ordinary times—normal times, when I should be happy—I felt lost.

TWO

Y OU LEARN THE world from your mother's face. You learn about God from the way she moves, how she loves or doesn't love, how she smells, what she says in words and silence. You learn about creation from the way your parents love each other, the story they tell you about how they came together to make you. These details create your idea of who you are and where you came from, the color, texture, depth, or shallowness of your universe, the particular tangle of roots that brought you out of the ground.

On the afternoon that I was conceived, my mother was sitting on a lawn chair on Fairfax Avenue in Los Angeles, smoking a Pall Mall and wondering what a woman with legs as good as hers was doing in a boardinghouse at twenty-nine, already divorced, with two young daughters to take care of and no romantic prospects at all. Ida and the girls—Marcia, eight, and Joyce, a year younger—had recently said good-bye to Pelham Parkway in the Bronx and boarded a train west to California, where my aunt and grandfather were already living, to start a new life. In the weeks since she'd arrived, my mother had fallen completely in love with this land of eternal summer, where the air smelled of orange blossoms instead of factory smoke, where women in scarves and sunglasses sped by in convertibles, and where no one knew her reputation. Here my mother hoped to meet a man better than the one she'd left behind, who'd beaten her up when he found her cheating—which was often—until finally she admitted that she didn't really love the slob and escaped down the tenement stairs with their girls.

My mother was looking at her legs now, browning in the sun—perfectly shaped, not too thin—and feeling lonely, wanting to be touched. My mother needed to be touched often, by many men. She'd developed this habit when she was a teenager and nature blessed (and cursed) a thirteen-year-old girl with the sudden appearance of breasts so big they belonged on a seven-foot woman—showgirl breasts, E cup, with nipples as big as tennis balls. My mother became an overnight sensation on Pelham Parkway; the boys, especially the Italian hoods who passed by her father's kosher dairy store, leering in the windows—and later, their brothers, cousins, uncles, fathers—couldn't wait to get a look at Ida Kaplan's chest—or a feel, which they copped every chance they could, with or without my mother's consent. "They wouldn't leave me alone," my mother used to tell me, her voice mixed with pride and sadness. In time, she grew to like the attention, to crave it; in time, she came to think of herself as little more than those breasts, a walking TOUCH ME sign for any horny man with fingers, Ida the Tits flaunting herself in hopes that out of all these animals, one would turn out to love her.

None of them did. It was 1940 and no one wanted a girl like that for more than twenty minutes. My little Polish grandma, Bella, who loved both her daughters—but, good Ruthie more—wrung her hands as she watched my mother throw herself away. When Bella tried to reason with Ida, telling her to save herself for her husband, my mother sneered. On a family outing to Coney Island when my mother was fifteen, drawing wolf whistles and stares from men on the boardwalk, Ida turned to her mother, sticking out her chest and tossing her thick brunette hair like Rita Hayworth, and asked how it felt to have a daughter as beautiful as she was.

"Beauty fades," my grandma told her, but Ida didn't care. When my Russian grandpa, Sidney, tried locking her in her room at night, my mother snuck down the fire escape in her high heels, into the tattooed arms of one of her favorite thugs. "I always went for the bad boys," she told me when she recounted these stories later, when her looks were gone and my father had left. As a little boy, it was hard for me to picture this prematurely old woman—with her hollow cheeks and sad eyes, chewed fingernails, and hair combed back like a man's— ever being pretty and young, but photographs showed me that my mother had really been a bombshell once. And on one of those days when she was twenty-nine—sitting on the front lawn of a boarding-house on Fairfax Avenue in May 1956, studying the shape of her legs while Marcia and Joyce played hopscotch in the hot afternoon sun— she saw my father for the first time.

He was six feet tall and slim as a whip, with big arms, greased-back black hair, and gray eyes like a wolf's. His face was angular, like mine, but the chin was square, with a cleft in it deep enough to hold a quarter. My mother watched him get out of his pickup truck, cig-arette between his teeth, grab his toolbox from the back, and come striding across the lawn in her direction. His overalls told her he was a fix-it man, and when their eyes met, my mother smiled and held his stare as my father tipped his chin to say hello.

He was a drifter, living off odd jobs, trying to stay sober. That after-noon, he was there to fix one of the bathroom pipes, as my mother found out when she meandered inside a few minutes later and found him on all fours under the upstairs sink, knocking a wrench against the enamel. Seeing the sweat soaking through the back of his shirt, she offered to get him a Coke. When she handed him the bottle, my father made sure his fingers brushed hers, and when she was about to leave, he asked her to keep him company while he worked. My mother sat on the toilet and watched him fiddling with the plumbing—and sneaking looks, which she caught, at her breasts nearly falling out of her sundress—her mouth painted soft orange like the inside of a cantaloupe.

When he gently kicked the door shut and pulled my mother down on the tile next to him, she didn't try to stop him, and in that hour of fabulous lust, my life began.

The attraction between my parents was strong enough to get them to the altar before I was born, but by that time the marriage was already a wreck. In addition to his heavy drinking, my father was a liar, as my mother discovered when his fabrications (mostly over what had happened to his paycheck) snow-balled into absurdity and fell apart. He was also tough on Marcia and Joyce, who worshipped and feared him, and on Ida, who was soon up to her old tricks, flirting with other men. There were vicious fights, threats to leave or call the cops. Still, my mother hoped that the marriage would hang together somehow, and when she heard "It's a boy" through her twilight sleep, and the doctor laid my newborn body across her breast, my mother wept for joy, feeling in her Jewish bones that she'd finally done something right, that a son might keep my father from leaving her.

At first, it almost seemed to work. I was the golden boy that both my parents dreamed of having. My father adored me and set about trying to turn me into the kind of rough-and-tumble son the average American dad wanted in the 1950s: riding shotgun in his pickup, my hair greased into a pompadour, just like his. My mother, who began to notice as soon as I could talk that I was unusual—precocious, inquisitive, and slightly girlish—hoped that my father wouldn't mind these slight deviations, and he didn't, apparently, bragging to the neighbors that he had a genius son who memorized an entire Dr. Seuss book at two. For a couple of years, we were a happyish family, despite the fact that there was no money ("The boss broke his hand and couldn't sign the checks!" my father claimed). Marcia and Joyce adjusted to their stepfather's temper; my mother did her best to make a home—though nesting didn't come naturally to her. Even after my sister Bella came along, when I was three, I remained the center of the household, making everybody shake their heads at my antics— "Where did you *come* from?" my mother would ask me often—the demon-child mascot that no one could control.

Uncontrollable, too, was my mother's need for romance, and shortly after Belle was born, Ida started flirting with the wrong man, or rather, the *right* man, the one she'd been waiting her whole life to meet, the only man—as she told us later—she'd ever truly loved. His name was Willy; he was a friend of the family and married himself. It wasn't long before my father got wind of the affair and threatened to kill Willy and my mother both if they didn't lay off. They tried not to see each other, but did anyway, and finally—after months of my mother's lies and my father's rage, nightlong marathons of violence that left Marcia, Joyce, and me huddling together in the bedroom closet, covering our ears—my father stormed out of the house with his suitcase.

"Why don't you just stop?" I begged my mother.

She looked at me, four years old, always asking questions about things she didn't think I understood, and shook her head. "I can't, honey," is all she said. "It's not my fault."

Weeks passed, I missed my father, blamed my mother, and waited every day for him to come back for me. I'd sit by the living room window and listen for the sound of his truck in the driveway—like when he used to come home from work—the familiar slam of his car door, when I'd run outside and throw myself at him, anxious to tell him all the crazy things I'd done that day and have him toss me in the air.

The day he finally did come back, it was already dark outside. Belle was in her crib; Marcia, Joyce, and I were sitting in front of the TV set; my mother was down the block at Rose Guttman's playing calookie. I heard the truck pull into the driveway and ran to the window, screaming, "Daddy!" but when I went to open the door, Marcia threw herself in front of it and bolted it shut instead.

"Call Mommy!" she yelled at Joyce, holding my hands behind my back while I struggled to break free. Marcia had orders not to let my father back into the house, and when he knocked on the door, shouting, "Let me in, goddammit!" Marcia begged him to please go away.

"I came for Mark," he said through the door.

I twisted and tried to bite Marcia's hand, but she held me tight. "I'm here!" I yelled. "Don't leave!" Somehow I managed to break away and turn the doorknob, and in a flash, my father grabbed me and started running out toward the truck, holding me close to his face, his beard scratching my cheek, his hair oil smelling like mayonnaise. We were moving fast, almost inside, when I heard my mother's heels on the sidewalk.

"Put him down!" she screamed; then she was there, her hands coiled around my ankles, trying to yank me out of my father's arms. He tightened his grip on my wrists, she squeezed my ankles even harder, and they stood there in the beam of the headlights, pulling me apart, ripping my pajamas, and snarling at each other like mad dogs while I felt myself splitting down the middle. Finally my mother kicked my father in the shin and he dropped me on the pavement.

Ida grabbed my hand and dragged me twisting and screaming into the house and locked the door.

I ran to the window and saw my father leaning against his truck in silhouette, rubbing his shin. Marcia tried to coax me away, but I held to the venetian blinds, my face pushed against the pane. I watched my father turn and get back into his truck. He started the motor and honked the horn—once, as if to signal me—then he slowly backed out of the driveway. I watched the headlights bounce when he hit the street, then turn and disappear.

I never saw or heard from him again.

Half of me left with my father that night; half of me slipped out of my mother's house, stayed in his arms, hit the road, while the other part—a strange, skinny, fair-haired boy—was trapped in a house full of sad, dark women. I couldn't understand why I'd been marooned in this place, why everything around me seemed so desolate and broken.

After my father left, my mother no longer tried to hide her affair with Willy; every Tuesday night for the next fourteen years, unless someone was sick or had died, her lover would pull up to the curb in front of our apartment building and honk the horn of his Lincoln Continental. My mother, who'd been waiting nervously all day, would kiss us good-bye and walk quickly out of the house—perfumed, hair done, teetering on her four-inch mules—carrying her little straw valise. The four of us would stand huddled together in front of the window and watch her throw her arms around Willy's neck the minute she slid into the car. When she came back the next morning, disheveled, exhausted, and depressed, we knew that the rest of the week would be hell, my mother slumping around in her nightgown, soaking for hours in the bathtub, smoking cigarettes, barely paying attention to us, while Marcia—by then in her early teens—went about the business of running the family and trying to keep the landlord off our backs.

My father had left us without a penny, and though my mother succeeded in getting us on welfare, there was barely enough to pay the rent and keep us fed and clothed. One day the electricity would be turned off and we'd be eating hot dogs by candlelight; the next week, Sears Roebuck would show up to repossess our furniture, leaving us to sit on the floor. We lived in three small rooms, Marcia and Joyce in one bedroom, Belle, my mom and I in the other. The rent was $95 a month—a sum my mother could never let us forget, wringing her hands, trying to figure out how to pay it—and from month to month we didn't know whether or not we'd be thrown out on the street. My mother blamed "the son of a bitch," reminding me again and again how lucky I was that my father had gone away—claiming I wasn't the boy he wanted anyway—drilling it into my head until I almost began to believe her.

Every day except Tuesday, the house was thick with my mother's gloom, the venetian blinds drawn, the musty rooms she didn't clean smelling of cat shit, tobacco, and Aqua Net hairspray. Six mornings a week, I opened my eyes half-expecting Ida to be dead. I'd wake up in hot, piss-soaked sheets and look over at her bed in the dark, where she lay smoking a cigarette. I'd fix my eyes on the ash, and when it changed color as she inhaled, glowing orange to yellow-white, I knew that she was still breathing.

As children, we did our best to help my mother bear her grief, but nothing we did could take it away; no amount of obedience on Marcia's part, antics on mine, sheer adorability on Belle's, could lift the sourness from our mother's spirit or spur her to take care of us. Joyce didn't even try. She was always my mother's nemesis, a belligerent, stubborn girl who ate herself up to 325 pounds and bossed the rest of us around like a tyrant. We couldn't walk down the street without being taunted. "Freak show!" the kids would yell at horse-faced Marcia, blubbery Joyce, and me, the green-eyed little fairy, as we passed by on our way to school.

When Joyce was fifteen, she got herself pregnant, but she was already so big that nobody knew it till she was practically in labor. When our mother found out, she sent Joyce to a home for unwed mothers, and when the baby girl was born, Ida insisted that she be put up for adoption. Two years later, Joyce met Johnny, a blue-collar trucker nearly as big as she was, and married him. Her second child was born a few months later, a boy this time, named Brian—and, for a brief moment, with a ring on her finger, a man who was kind to her, and a son, it almost seemed, as it had when my mother gave birth to me, that Joyce could turn her jinxed life around. When Brian was born, my hard-luck sister was happy for the first time that I could remember.

This happiness ended three weeks later. On my way home from school, I turned the corner behind the liquor store and crossed the alley behind our building to Wilkinson, our street, and stopped in my tracks. Something was obviously wrong: cars were parked by our building that didn't belong there, my aunt Ruth's blue Corvair, my grandpa's beige Impala, Joyce and Johnny's pickup truck.

I ran into the house. A crowd of friends and the whole family were sitting in our dark living room—except Joyce, whom I could hear sobbing behind the closed bathroom door. No one said a word to me when I entered; they just sat there, frozen. There were nuts and orange jelly candies in the lazy Susan—I'd never seen anything there before. I grabbed a handful and asked my aunt Ruth, "What's wrong?"

She took my hand and pulled me to her, stroking my head. "I'm not a kid," I said, though I was only eight. "Tell me, Aunt Ruthie."

"Honey," she said, but before she could finish her sentence, the bathroom door opened and Joyce came out, looking wild with pain, her hair stuck to the sweat on her face, cheeks red and wet, vacant eyes. Johnny went to put his arm around her, but she pushed him away and looked at me.

"Go ahead," Joyce cried. "Tell him."

Aunt Ruthie turned me to her and held both my hands. Her eyes were brown with a white-blue rim, like my mother's, only softer. "Brian's gone, honey," she said. That morning, Joyce had found Brian in his crib, limp, blue, mysteriously dead.

Every day, it seemed, something terrible happened in our family—something bloody or bizarre—things that didn't happen in other people's houses. There was no order or sense where we lived, as if we were caught in a twilight zone. Within these shadows, bad things happened that made the world seem a heartless place. "It's a stinking life," my mother used to say. "No one's gonna be there to protect you."

Death, or the threat of it, was always close by, hovering in the background. You could smell it when you crossed our doorstep, the danger, the sense that in this little apartment, with the ratty furniture and empty cupboards, life was barely supportable and anything could happen. One day we came home and found a litter of kittens drowned in the bathtub by our upstairs neighbors; another day, the lunatic crone next door was swinging a length of chain at my mother out back by the trash cans. On any given night, after Johnny divorced her, some guy might be chasing Joyce around the house shouting, "I ain't gonna rape you, baby"; another evening, there was a gunshot, stomping feet, and screams. The year I started kindergarten, I was hit by a semi truck in the street, my right foot smashed like hamburger.

When she was thirteen, Belle, who was visiting a ranch where they trained animals for the movies, stuck her hand in a tiger's cage and was mauled, two of her fingers stripped of flesh, afterward twisted and purple like claws. After that, the little girl who had been my pet—a spindly legged version of me—the sweet, skinny monkey I adored and who, in our father's absence, looked to me for care and protection, was changed almost overnight to a teenage girl with lines in her face and loose habits like our mother's. Nothing I said could convince Belle that she still mattered—not with her ugly hand. She dropped out of school and started hanging around with the low riders on Van Nuys Boulevard, who kept her busy running back and forth to the abortion clinic. Nothing I did could protect her from a world that ruined innocent things or from the legacy of my mother's sadness.

One day, when I was seven, I was sitting in my favorite spot on the living room rug, staring into the gray-brown weave, waiting for my mother to get out of the tub. She was always in there a long time, but that day it seemed like hours. I knew better than to rush her, so I waited in my spot, bored, playing with the bobby pins and cat hair.

When I first heard thumping, I thought it was my imagination. Then I heard it again, coming from the bathroom. I went to the door and tried to turn the knob, but it was locked.

"Mommy?" I said. She didn't answer. "Mommy?" I said again, louder. Again there was no response—just a thumping sound, *whomp, whomp,* like a fist.

"Mommy, come out!" I shouted, but the noise didn't stop. I could hear her sobbing and moaning, whispering, "I want to die."

I kicked the door and screamed at her to come out. The more she thumped, the more I kicked. Then the thumping suddenly stopped. I heard the water sloshing; the door opened. My mother was there with a towel around her, dripping on the floor, staring at me with dead eyes. A stream of blood trickled down her neck from behind her ear, where she had been hitting her head against the enamel.

Marcia did what she could to comfort me. My oldest sister worked hard to fill in the gaps my mother left, to do the small things for me and Belle that make children feel like children, reading us stories from Aesop and O. Henry, taking us to play in the park, cooking us special foods we liked. Marcia was a ray of kindness in this nightmare, a lonely, pockmarked girl who worked hard at school for average grades and suffered at the hands of her critical mother and unhappy sister.

From the time Marcia was a teenager, the signs were there that something was wrong. Often she'd spend sunny days buried beneath her bedcovers, the blinds drawn tight. After she got her own apartment, she'd come back to visit me. On one of these visits, looking bereft, her hair dirty, her blouse stained, she asked me, "How do you do it, Mark?"

"Do what?" I asked.

"Live," she answered. Though I was nine years younger, Marcia always seemed to look up to me. She admired my independence, she said, and the way I didn't take no for an answer.

"You just *do*," I told her, but that didn't seem to help at all. As the years went by, Marcia got worse, sadder and unable to care for herself in the most basic ways. Some mornings, it was more than she could manage to get out of bed, take a shower, and get to work. She was too raw even to read a newspaper; tragic headlines the rest of us took in stride left Marcia terrified and depressed. She seemed to have no filter, or armor, and the anguish this caused her became a kind of madness. One day she admitted to me that she'd gone to the roof of the bank building where she worked during her lunch hour and sat with her legs dangling over the edge, wondering how it would feel to jump.

I tried to understand her—more than that, I tried to help Marcia understand herself and why she felt bound for self-destruction. Sometimes my pep talks worked for a while. She'd lose weight, find a new job, a new man, a new way to fight her demons; then they'd pin her down again. The flatness would creep back into her voice, and she'd call me in the middle of the night, afraid of herself, begging me to help her.

When she finally cracked, after an ugly divorce, and was put into an institution, Marcia seemed surprisingly relieved. She didn't have to worry there, she told us when we visited. The doctors understood her fears; they understood that she couldn't make the pain go away. And there, in the safety of the hospital, Marcia believed she could rest until she was stronger.

After only a month, however, the insurance company insisted on sending her home. Marcia might not be cured, they concluded, but at least she posed no immediate danger to society. "I'm not ready," Marcia insisted when we went to pick her up, pleading with our mother to talk to the doctors and somehow convince them to let her stay. Ida told her it was time to buck up.

Fifteen days later, Belle found Marcia's body. She was already unconscious—asleep, Belle thought at first, until she saw the empty pill bottles. She called the ambulance, but Marcia was brain dead by the time paramedics got there. Still, they admitted her to the ICU, propped up her body in a glass cubicle, and for the next three days, the legal waiting period in California, Marcia lay there naked to the waist, tubes in her nose, machines beeping all around her. For three long terrible days, Joyce, Belle, Ida, and I sat in the hospital cafeteria playing rummy, waiting for it to be over. Every time a code blue was announced over the loudspeaker, Ida grabbed my hand and told me to run upstairs to see if the end had come. Inside the cubicle, doctors and nurses would be pounding on Marcia's chest, trying to resuscitate her, leaving her skin black and blue.

"No more! Please," I begged them, but they wouldn't stop the assaults. As soon as the peaks and valleys on the cardiograph reappeared, the cubicle would empty as quickly as it had filled. My mother would run a comb through Marcia's hair, staring at her body in disbelief.

You learn the world from your mother's face. The bottomless grief in Ida's eyes told me that the world was cruel to its core, that *this* is what happened to good people. Her stony look let me know that if I was to survive, I'd have to toughen up now, break the world before it broke me, realize, without whining, that justice was simply out of the question.

THREE

A FEW WEEKS after my twenty-eighth birthday, my college buddy John and I flew down to Jamaica for a week of cruising and oblivion. John was my partner in bitching, a willing victim—as a high-priced attorney—to the same golden-handcuff syndrome I found myself in. Our lives had run uncannily parallel courses since our undergraduate days at Berkeley, and after a brief affair, we'd trailed each other through grad school and east to New York, through the suspense of the job hunt, the thrill of being hired, the climb in our respective offices, and the precipitous fall into disillusionment. Most of our time together was spent propping up each other's morale, commiserating and plotting our escape.

Jamaica had been John's idea. On the plane down, he told me, again, how unhappy he was with life in an Armani suit.

"The other day I was coming out of my office at the end of the day," he said, flagging down the steward for a second Bacardi. "I got to the top of the escalator and looked down. All I saw were thousands of suits and ties going up and down, up and down—a *mass* of them, like automatons. It scared the shit out of me. I felt like somebody had drained me out of myself, like *Invasion of the Body Snatchers*." John hissed and made that horrible face that Donald Sutherland makes at the end of the movie. "Like really *evil*."

"You've always been evil."

"Not me. Them. Oh, thank you." John took the drink from the cute steward and stuffed a five-dollar bill into his hip pocket. "Not bad," he said, staring at the boy's butt as he pushed his food cart down the aisle. "Anyway, I've got to get out of there. It's imperative."

At the hotel, we bought a bag of ganja from the pool man and prepared ourselves for a week of bliss. Every morning we'd sip coffee under the palm trees on our terrace; in the afternoons, we'd grease ourselves up in our Speedos and watch gorgeous Rastafarians strut by, leering at us with strange yellow eyes, flexing their muscles and stamping the sand like bulls protecting their territory. With each successive day of collapse, the Caribbean effect (overradiated-coconut-oil stupor) would melt a little more of my brains—almost enough to give me the illusion of happiness.

John was undemanding company, my opposite in nearly every way. He was soft spoken, loose limbed, kind, extremely cool. I judged everyone and everything instantly, rarely compromised and spent most of my time feeling borderline combustible. Still the chemistry between us was effortless, and the week passed without disagreement. John met up with an old lover, a sexy, pint-sized Australian who took him for midnight rides on the back of his motorcycle. I resigned myself to the fact that none of the Rastafarians had any interest whatever in swinging my way, and spent my nights writing in my journal, trying to circle into myself, to loosen the fist of intense feelings still clutching my gut.

Our last morning on the island, I left the hotel early and set out alone toward the beach, with nothing more serious on my mind than sand, sea, and ganja-smoking boys in tight tropical shorts. A short distance down a dirt road lined with thirty-foot palms, I suddenly stopped dead in my tracks, without knowing why. Something about the picture in front of me—a white sandy path extending a mile between rows of perfectly spaced, monumental palms—froze me and made the hair on my arms stand on end. It wasn't the postcard beauty; the power was more mysterious and disturbing than that. I stood there completely still, absorbing the details of the place—the hot, wet smell of jungle morning, sweet with papaya and star fruit, the caw of parrots and the buzz of mosquitos, the palm fronds swaying against a crystalline sky—and felt overwhelmed by an unmistakable sense that something was about to change my life.

When John joined me later at the beach, I said nothing. He stretched out next to me, bony and bronzed, closing his eyes, puffing on a cigarette and smiling to the sound of music coming through his Walkman—soprano Elisabeth Schwarzkopf singing Strauss's *Four Last Songs*. I could hear the sad, thin thread of her voice leaking out of the headphones and followed it with my eyes down John's body, from the neck to the clavicle, down into the strange indentation, big as an orange, that dipped between his pecs, to the golden hair along his flat stomach, across the fuchsia rayon of his suit to his skinny legs.

Watching him, I felt a glow of comrade love. Our lives had been so unintentionally bound for so many years. I'd watched him evolve from a punk-rock undergrad to hotshot attorney earning six figures. I'd nursed him through half a dozen doomed love affairs. I felt, in that moment, closer to John than to anyone else in my life. I reached over and touched the dip in his chest, where a pool of sweat had formed. He smiled without opening his eyes, wrapped his fingers around mine, and sucked on his Marlboro.

"Happy?" I asked.

"Very."

I closed my eyes and drifted, dreaming of a flock of squawking birds. When I looked up a few minutes later, I found that we were

31

surrounded by a group of local teenage girls, begging us to buy their wares, conch shells etched with palm trees, hats woven from fronds, bead necklaces, and ankle bracelets. We tried to shoo them away, but they wouldn't budge. The girls were the color of nougat, and they slid up next to us on our towels, deliberately hiking up their skirts to show us their white cotton panties and butt cheeks encrusted with sand. They giggled and cooed, and when we refused to cough up American dollars, attacked our heads, despite our protests, with colored beads and barrettes, twisting our hair into cornrows. Flashing white teeth, they licked their lips and surveyed our bodies shamelessly. The prettiest among them ran her fingernail down John's neck, shoulders, nipples, then put her mouth next to his ear, ogling the bulge in his bathing suit.

"Jamaican girls like the big bamboo," she said. John and I were in convulsions. She took his foot between her hands and pulled at the long toes, counting little piggies. When she turned his foot in my direction, I saw, halfway between the ball and the heel, a purple spot the size of a dime that hadn't been there the day before.

Lives, like buildings, have foundation walls. Take out that crucial beam and the whole thing comes crashing down around your ears. In the instant that I saw John's lesion, in the seconds it took me to realize what it was and what it meant for both of us, life as I'd known it cracked down the middle, from chimney to basement. The house I'd lived in—the self I'd believed in, the future I'd thought was waiting for me—was suddenly condemned.

Though it was John's foot and not mine, I knew without question that the virus was in me. There was almost nothing I hadn't done. I'm one of the lucky people who remembers what sex was like in 1975, perhaps the last time in the history of human intercourse when semen was a prize, not a poison, a secret, salty swap of the very thing that made you a man. Sex as I'd lived it, through two voracious decades, was a drug that left no headache, a gentleman's addiction, always available, always gratifying, always a lift for my spirits. In a painful and uncertain world, sex was the thing I could count on, a game I could always win, where I could be as crazy as I liked and feel, for an hour's time, a measure of freedom from myself.

With the first reports of a new venereal syndrome, I assumed that the Angel of Death had not passed over my house. Still, that was abstract information until this moment, when a half inch of purple skin hit me right between the eyes like a sniper's bullet. If the ticking clock had already become audible with the first reports, John's lesion amplified its sound by a thousand, drawing it out of the middle distance and into the radius of my intimate life.

Lying there on the beach in silence once the girls had gone, too terrified to show the lesion to John, I realized something else, too. I suddenly knew that as frightened as I was to die, I was equally scared of dying *this* way—as the person I was at that moment, cynical and profoundly lost. Miserable as it would undoubtedly be to discover a lesion on my skin some morning, it would be much worse—twice as bad, it seemed to me—to face that catastrophe with no idea who I was or why I was put here, where I was headed, what, if anything, this life meant. Stumbling off this cliff like a sleepwalker who had never opened his eyes seemed like a fate worse than dying young.

This thought seized me and wouldn't let go. I needed to know, or at least to ask, if there was anything beyond our bodies—a soul, a spirit, a banger of the big bang? Was there a source of something "else" inside us—something *meta*physical—or were we, as I'd been raised to believe, dying animals like a billion others, biological blips on the screen of a heartless creation, born to eat and fuck and die?

Everything looked suddenly different after that day, temporary, booby-trapped, even the green waves eating away at the shore. John and I had told ourselves that there would be plenty of time in the future to find *meaning* in our lives, once the student loans were paid off, our apartments decorated, all our worldly whims satisfied. We had comforted ourselves with the not unreasonable belief for men under thirty that there would be time for such abstract pursuits later on. Now, I saw that this was a lie; John and I were probably dying, trapped together in a closed room getting smaller—and there was not a minute to waste. I realized with a shudder, like someone shaken awake by an explosion, that I would exit this world as lost as I was at that moment if I didn't do something to change very fast.

FOUR

O N T H E M O R N I N G of March 1, 1986, shortly after my return from Jamaica, I was at my desk sorting through the day's mail when I came across the galleys of a novel that looked interesting. It was a story, I deduced from the flap copy, of three characters in Paris (two of whom happened to be gay) searching for spiritual strength in a tough, sophisticated world. I was immediately struck by the eloquence of the prose and how closely aspects of this story reflected my own dilemma.

I learned from the author's biography that he had been born in India and schooled in England, and at thirty-three had already written ten books. Scanning the jacket photo of a melancholy, bespectacled man with a mop of curls, I decided that *Interview*'s crew of hair and makeup people could probably render Alexander Maxwell sufficiently attractive for profile standards, and I called his publisher to request an interview. As it turned out, he was in New York promoting the novel, and we arranged a meeting for the following week.

My customary interviewing bravado had done nothing to prepare me for the character who appeared in the doorway of my office just before two o'clock on the appointed afternoon.

"This hateful city!" he snarled. "It is truly is the end of civilization as we've known it."

I laughed. "Excuse me?"

"Sorry," Alexander Maxwell said, taking off his glasses and rubbing his eyes. They were sad like a spaniel's eyes, brown, with dark rings under them and a strange fold at the inner corner that made him look simultaneously like an idiot, a genius, and an alien. The rest of his face looked exhausted and extremely beautiful, thin and pale as a cameo, with tight, hurt lips. He was dressed from head to toe in black, and a wild mane of dark hair was standing out from his head like the feathers of an electrocuted crow.

"I'm so sorry, I've had a difficult day," he apologized again, smoothing his hair with the palms of his hands and trying to smile. "Every time I come to New York, I feel like I'm being disemboweled." Alexander paused and looked at me to determine whether or not to continue.

"Please," I said, turning on the tape recorder.

"When I was a child, I once saw a panther skinned in the marketplace. The wretched man dragged it behind him on a bicycle, bloody and still alive. I will never forget that panther's howling." The strange man on the other side of my desk closed his eyes and contorted his face. "Do you know the story of Goethe losing his mind at the sight of a horse being flayed?"

"No."

"I often feel that way myself," said Alexander, "as if the cruelty of this world would shatter any sensitive being who actually looked at it. Don't you agree?"

I was out of my depth. "The world is cruel," I agreed. "But I'm not sure that it's ever been any different."

Alexander looked me straight in the eyes. "That's where you're wrong," he said. "The world is much worse than it's ever been. We're at the end of an entire cycle of history, you know."

I glanced at the spindle on the tape recorder to make sure that it was turning. "Is that right?" I asked. "Please. Go on."

Alexander reached forward and pressed the button to stop the tape. "Do you always humor people this way?" he asked, leaning back in his chair and folding his arms across the front of his blazer.

"I'm sorry. I wasn't aware that I was humoring you."

"Please," he said. "I don't have time for games. Particularly with handsome men." Alexander Maxwell looked at me again, smirking this time. "You're very handsome, you know."

"Thank you," I said, turning the tape recorder back on. "So are you."

"I'm not everybody's cup of tea," he said, chuckling. "But I'm some people's liqueur." Then he leaned toward me across the desk and stared deep into my eyes. "Green," he said. "I should have known."

"Known what?" I asked, trying to follow his quicksilver mind.

Alexander smiled to himself. "Nothing," he said, still smirking at me.

"You were saying?"

"Right. The apocalypse," Alexander said. "How much time do we have, anyway? Twenty years at the most? Everyone must now admit that the end is in sight. 'Work now, for the night is coming,' it says in Ecclesiastes." Alexander paused again, then reached out and turned off the tape recorder. "Do you mind if I ask you a personal question?"

"Not at all."

"Are you ill?"

Inwardly, I gasped. No one had ever asked me that question before, and now, hearing it out of the mouth of a total stranger, I was shocked, my gut seized up tight as a drum. I avoided Alexander's eyes, fidgeted in my chair, trying not to let him see that I suddenly couldn't breathe. Finally, with as much cool as I could fake, I answered, "No, I'm not. At least not as far as I know."

Alexander scrutinized me, seemingly unconvinced. "It's dangerous out there, you know."

"Believe me, I do." I hadn't stopped thinking about John's lesion for five minutes. "What made you think I was ill?"

"You look a little peaked."

"I thought you said I was cute," I teased, trying not to sound offended.

"What *is* the matter with you then?" asked Alexander, a look of genuine concern on his face.

"Maybe it's stress," I answered.

"It's more than that," he said.

"Wait a minute," I said, disoriented by how quickly Alexander had turned the tables. "*I'm* supposed to be asking the questions. Besides," I said, genuinely curious. "How do you *know* all this?"

"I'm not blind, for God's sake," said Alexander. Then he sighed and fished a piece of ice from his Perrier, sliding it in circles around the corners of his eyes, as if putting out a fire. "I see things," he said. "Like Cassandra. Only people hardly ever believe me."

"I believe you," I said tentatively, "but what do you see?"

Alexander popped the ice cube into his mouth and gazed at me for a few more seconds. "Do you really want to know?"

I nodded.

"All right. The world is on fire. The things that genuinely matter—truth, beauty, honor, spirit—are all in ruins. And here you sit, a young man obviously at some kind of crossroads, at the very core of the inferno, slaving for the devil himself."

Again, he took my breath away. How many times had I watched Warhol waft by my office, ghostlike, his sharp dead eyes surveying his kingdom, and felt an actual chill pass through me? How often had I secretly wondered whether Andy wasn't really the Antichrist—not Andy the man, of course, but Andy the symbol—a clever fraud feeding off the entrails of capitalism like a hyena? How often had I wondered, finally, what this equation said about me, and whether I hadn't made a pact with the devil by becoming one of his lackeys.

Though I'd thought this many times before, I'd never articulated it quite so bluntly or heard it said by anyone else. Sitting there with a man I hardly knew, I felt for the first time that someone was finally speaking the truth. "I can't believe you said that," I finally answered.

"It's rare to meet someone who tells the truth," Alexander replied quickly, as if he had picked up my thought. "How have you managed to survive?"

"By the skin of my teeth. The rewards, I guess."

"Dinner with Liz. Limousines. The envy of friends you haven't the vaguest respect for. The lubricated strokes of maya."

"Maya?"

"The Sanskrit word for illusion—the appearance, the reflection in the mirror, everything that a culture that has banned mystical knowledge in favor of godlessness insists upon calling reality."

"You're losing me."

"Don't worry, I lose everyone. Sooner or later." Alexander reached out and patted my hand. "You'll understand what I'm talking about soon enough. In the meantime, tell me about yourself."

"You're forgetting that I'm here to interview you."

"Woo me first, then you can suck my blood," Alexander said, throwing back his head with a frightening cackle. "That reminds me. Did you hear what Anita Bryant said about fellatio? Speaking of vampires! Could you choke? What *will* you Americans think of next?"

So our first encounter went, with Alexander slipping from the sublime to the raunchy, the personal to the grandiose, the classical to a camp hysteria so flamboyant and so infectious that I finally shut my office door so the rest of the staff couldn't eavesdrop. I was captivated and stimulated by Alexander Maxwell; he was completely unlike anyone or anything I'd come across before, almost as if he belonged to a different breed or species. I realized immediately that whatever this power was that radiated out of him, whatever gave him the courage to say such bold and truthful things, I wanted it.

Our meeting lasted for two hours. When Alexander finally left my office, kissing me French-style, on both cheeks, he promised that we would meet again very soon. Afterward, I was as exhilarated as if I'd touched a live wire, charged with the unmistakable sense that in this man I'd met my match. His presence filled me with hyperbole: it was like hearing Beethoven after a lifetime of Muzak, opening the window and seeing a Monet landscape after twenty-eight years trapped inside a Francis Bacon. After he'd gone, my hearing felt sharper, my vision more focused; some latent force inside me had jolted to attention.

"He sounds completely crazy," Carole declared that evening.

My best friend was jealous of Alexander before she'd even met him. This didn't surprise me. Carole was jealous of everyone in my life who wasn't her. We were each other's linchpin to survival, our main squeeze without the squeeze. Carole and I had spanned the archetypes of every primal relationship that a woman in her forties and a gay man of twenty-eight could have—father-daughter, mother-son, sister-brother, husband-wife. Now she was trying, as she always did, to protect me from the unknown, namely Alexander Maxwell and the dangerous fire he appeared to have lit underneath me.

"He *is* crazy," I tried to explain. "But in an amazing way that's saner than anyone I've ever met."

"That's what they said about Jim Jones."

"Don't start."

"Never trust people who rant about God."

"He didn't rant, he rhapsodized. And he didn't mention God."

"Whatever you want to call it." At heart, Carole was a Catholic girl and on top of her pope-induced frigidity, and a mortal terror of turning on a spit in hell, she did not respond well to free thinking.

"It's called passion," I said.

"It's called fanaticism."

"You may be right. But he moved me."

"Everything moves you for five minutes, then you start to hate it."

"That's the point: There's a hole in the bottom of me. I can't hold on to anything."

"You're just impulsive."

"I'm suicidal."

"Don't be ridiculous."

Carole and I had met three years before, on the island of Saint Martin. I had been invited there as part of a press junket to cover the First Celebrity Tennis Tournament in the Caribbean, a fiasco that began with a flourish of Dom Pérignon—and promises of Joan Collins, the bitch queen of the day, backhanding Linda Evans on the court—and ended with thirty-five sunburned editors twiddling their thumbs while Sonny Bono (one of the few celebrities who showed up) lobbed a ball back and forth with a pro.

One morning I went for a walk on the beach. It was another flawless, vacant Caribbean day, already hot at 8 A.M. I took off my shirt and walked for a mile or so, obsessing about the magazine, plotting how to charm Doris into giving me my next promotion. I visualized where I was on the masthead—down in the pits with the contributing editors—and where I wanted to be, right under the art director, and the thought of my name up there immediately lifted my spirits. I picked up my pace and started to jog in the surf, wrapping my shirt around my head to protect the bald spots, thinking about what a comer I was.

At that moment I heard a scream and snapped out of my reverie. "Uuuuh! Oy! Aaaah!" I turned around in the direction I'd just come and saw a woman tumbling in the waves, flailing and spluttering, caught in a curl. "Aaah!" she shouted again, spitting water from her mouth. "Oh, shit!" as the wave lifted her up and threw her down in the sand. I stopped and watched her trying to crawl out of the water on all fours, her hair full of sand and covering her face, only to be knocked down again by the next wave.

"Are you all right?" I asked.

"Oh yeah, just great." She was on her knees wiping caked sand from her lips and eyes. "A mermaid." She was a pretty woman in her forties, with auburn hair and freckles. She managed to stand up, and I gave her the shirt from my head to wipe the rest of the sand off her face. "Thank you," she said, avoiding my eyes. "Oh my God, how unbelievably *embarrassing*."

I looked at her standing there with her hair in a mop of sand and seaweed, skin mottled with debris, eyes confused. She saw me staring, and at that moment, the two of us burst into hysterics. We laughed for ten minutes—every time we stopped, we only had to look at each other to lose it again, like five-years-olds, until we didn't know what we were laughing about, only that we couldn't stop, bent over, clutching our bellies. "No more," I gasped, "no more. It hurts!" But that only made us laugh harder.

That's how our friendship began. In the years that followed, these conniptions would grip us mysteriously at any time, in any place, clinching a friendship that made no obvious sense. Carole and I had nothing in common. As I found out later that day, she'd recently left an alcoholic husband in New Jersey after twenty-five years of marriage and moved to Manhattan with her two college-aged daughters to start a new life. Carole was here on this junket only because a photographer friend brought her along as an assistant to promote her *Celebrity Buns Calendar*, featuring the ripe behinds of prominent soap opera stars.

Carole was a lonely, uneducated woman from the suburbs who liked sitcoms, lace curtains, and antiquing. She also, clearly, liked me, and this immediate, snowballing affection—which would come to border sometimes on romantic obsession—became both the trial and the glue of our strange friendship, sealed that day when Carole was washed up at my feet like a spastic Deborah Kerr.

Now, hearing me talk about Alexander Maxwell, Carole was dubious. "Just be careful," she said.

A few days after meeting Alexander, I found a package on my desk containing three books: an anonymous medieval tract called *The Cloud of Unknowing*, Satprem's *The Adventure of Consciousness*, and Rilke's *Letters to a Young Poet*, with the following section highlighted:

> That is at bottom the only courage that is demanded of us:
> to have courage for the most strange, the most singular and
> the most inexplicable that we may encounter. That mankind
> has in this sense been cowardly has done life endless harm;
> the experiences that are called "visions," the whole so-called
> "spirit world," death, all those things that are so closely akin to

us, have by daily parrying been so crowded out of life that the senses with which we could have grasped them are atrophied. To say nothing of God.

There was also a postcard of a Moghul painting showing a holy man in prayer. "The bird flies upward to its nest in light," was scrawled on the back of the card, alongside an invitation to join Alexander for lunch the following Saturday afternoon at the loft he had borrowed in Tribeca.

He came to the door in a black Armani dinner jacket, a scarlet shirt, and baggy trousers, tearing roughly at his wild hair with a pink plastic brush. Two pieces of toilet paper were stuck to his cheek and neck where he'd cut himself shaving. The loft was vast and white, and the voice of a soprano was blaring from the speakers. "Wonderful you're here!" he shouted.

"Let me guess!" I shouted back. "Maria Callas?"

"Second act of *Tosca*—where she drives the dagger into Scarpia." Alexander twisted his face, pulled an imaginary ring from his finger, flung it into space, and let his head fall to his shoulder, echoing Callas's wail with his own surprisingly limpid falsetto. "That is the cry of the ravaged feminine, of woman betrayed by masculine cruelty," Alexander said. "It's the story of our age, and Maria lived it like nobody else."

Alexander took me by the hand and led me to the sofa, sitting close enough for me to smell his aftershave.

"You don't seem to like men very much," I said.

"Oh, I *do*," Alexander insisted. "Or rather, I *would*, if they were real men. Unfortunately, most so-called men are really tyrannical little boys impersonating men. It's rare to meet a real man," Alexander said, turning and looking suggestively into my eyes. "Don't you find?"

"Depends on how hard you look," I answered.

He held my stare. "Really?"

"And where you're looking," I flirted.

"Aha. I see. You're a naughty boy."

"Man," I corrected.

"That remains to be seen." Alexander reached for a bottle of wine on the coffee table, filled two glasses, and handed one to me. "Here's to seeing," he said. "And to our new friendship." Alexander clinked his goblet against mine. "May you be as good as your word."

We drank and sat side by side on the sofa, listening to Callas sing. Alexander was visibly transported by the music and, when the aria was over, asked me what I thought of the diva's voice. "I find it threatening," I said.

"In what way?"

"It reminds me of my mother, I think."

"Oh my God," said Alexander. "From flirting to Freud in twenty seconds." We laughed and Alexander put his arm around my shoulders.

"Tell me something," I asked. "Why do you talk about masculine cruelty? Why not just say *human* cruelty?"

"Because women are not causing the destruction of life as we know it," he answered, turning to me. "I know that sounds harsh, but do you honestly think that in a world run by women, forty thousand children would die every day of preventable diseases while officials in the Pentagon masturbated over their disgusting toys?"

"You've got a point."

"It has nothing to do with not liking men. It's how men adapt to the world that makes me crazy. It's as if we believe that unless we kill what's tender in ourselves we can't succeed in the world. And that makes us cruel."

"So you include yourself in this?"

"Yes," said Alexander, "and no. I'm fairly androgynous, in case you hadn't noticed." This was true. While not effeminate, Alexander did seem to be an almost seamless mixture of male and female, a sort of hybrid defying conventional definition.

"Take yourself, for example," he continued. "You have an aching suspicion that you're wasting your life. Right?"

I didn't bother denying it, and simply nodded.

"And how does that feel?"

"Empty," I said. "Sometimes I feel kind of—"

"Dead?"

"Yes."

"Because you are," said Alexander. "Everyone is as long as they're trapped inside the ego. In Buddhist mythology there are characters known as hungry ghosts. Although these little trolls are starving, their mouths are the size of pinheads so they can't eat a thing at the feast around them. That's the meaning of depression."

"You know, until recently I'd never really thought of myself as depressed."

Alexander laughed. "People don't. That's the problem. So many people in this culture don't even *know* they're suicidal. That's because there are two kinds of depression. There's the dreary kind that everyone knows about—people who mope around, paralyzed—and then there are the triumphalists."

"And what exactly is a triumphalist?"

"An impostor." Alexander answered.

"So how do you know who is one and who isn't?"

"You measure a triumphalist's despair by his achievements. The more miserable he feels, the harder he works to cover it up. The more he hates himself, the more grandiose his goals become. Sound familiar?"

"Yes. But what's the solution?"

"Spiritual practice," he replied, pouring more wine into my glass. "Cheers."

"Cheers. But I don't really believe in God."

"Of course you don't. People like you never do."

"What does that mean?"

"You've got a head like a rock. I knew it the minute we met. You cynics need *experience*. Not religion, faith, or belief, but actual, quantifiable, incontestable, *personal* transcendental experience, in the body, with open eyes, in their ordinary lives. It will come."

"How do you know?"

"I told you. I'm Cassandra. But you must not give way to hopelessness. Feeling this deadness inside yourself, the intense hunger for something more, is the only way to start the journey. It's essential. Most of us must come to the end of our ropes, lose everything—or at least be at risk of losing everything—before we are willing to search for something else. Most of us have to exhaust every other road and be dragged to God kicking and screaming."

"What if we don't know what God is?"

"Find out," Alexander said. "Sooner or later, everyone faces the same choice. Start a new life or die in the one you have. Wake up or starve like a hungry ghost. This hunger you feel is latent in everyone, but most people wait till they're on their deathbed to face it. And then it's usually too late."

I automatically thought of John, already ill, completely unequipped to face his death, and felt again the piercing fear of ending up where he was, lost, without a clue as to what this all meant.

"Let me tell you a story," Alexander said gently, as if he could read my mind. "Once there was a family of frogs living at the bottom of a dark well. One day, one of the frogs escaped from the well and hopped all the way to the sea. When he beheld that expanse of blue as far as his frog eyes could see, he was stunned, overwhelmed. He hopped back to the well as fast as he could to tell the other froggies what he'd seen. They didn't believe him. They said, 'This well is all that's real, this little bit of mud and dirty water, this darkness, the slime, and the solid walls.' He tried and tried to convince them, but the frogs believed only in what they could see from their place at the bottom of the well.

"Finally, one of the frogs agreed to test his brother's claim and followed him up out of the well toward the sea. They hopped and hopped until they came to a ridge perched above the ocean. The second frog, whose eyes were accustomed to the dark, took one look at the enormous sea—the stupendous glittering expanse of water where waves rippled like jewels in the sunlight—and his head exploded."

I must have looked confused. Alexander smiled at me.

"We're all well frogs until we venture out, suspend our disbelief, and trust that there is more to life than meets the eye. It's the utmost stupidity and arrogance to believe that what the intellect perceives is the full range of human potential. The mind cannot register what is beyond the mind."

When he said this, I realized that it had never even occurred to me that there *was* anything beyond the mind.

"If we cling to what we know, nothing new can enter in."

"Maybe," I said. "But we need to use our minds too. We need to understand."

"To a point, yes. But there comes a phase when everybody must put aside what he knows and simply wait. Rilke describes it in the book I sent you."

48

"Where he talks about letting the questions rest, not jumping to conclusions." I'd devoured the book the day it arrived.

"Letting wisdom take root."

"I understand. But my trouble is that nothing takes root in me for very long."

"Because you're too quick to judge and discard what doesn't fit into your intellect. Almost everyone is these days. The tragedy of this is that none of the most sublime aspects of life, the things we yearn for the most, can be gained through analysis, any more than we can grip water between our fingers. Dissected by the mind, life is barren, fractured experience."

"I'm finding that out," I said. "You can say that again."

"And now," said Alexander, leaping up from the sofa, "it's time to go to the river." Alexander downed the rest of his wine and jumped to his feet, then pulled me up by the hand.

En route to the pier, we talked nonstop. Alexander seemed to be fascinated by my life, asking one question after another about my childhood, my fears, my dreams, my passions. The power of his curiosity was intoxicating; it excited me to be asked questions for a change, for someone to show such intense and astute interest in who I was. What's more, Alexander's responses impressed me; rather than shying away from the dark and dirty details (many of which I'd never told anyone before), he seemed actually to be drawn to the things that scared most people away.

For the next three hours, we sat with our legs dangling over the pier, gazing across the Hudson River at Hoboken, while I poured my heart out. Nothing I said seemed to shock or surprise Alexander; clearly, this was a man who'd battled his own demons already. It thrilled me finally to meet someone who seemed able to understand the whole, who might actually guide me and help me understand who I was and why I behaved as I did.

What Alexander wanted from me was obvious, too, as he took my hand and laced our fingers together, holding them up for me to see. I noticed for the first time that our hands were almost identical—wide palms, long thin fingers, knobby knuckles.

"You're the first man to interest me in a very long time," Alexander said, sounding awfully lonely. He confessed to me then that he'd never had what he called the "full experience," meaning love with a man who could return his love in body as well as in mind and spirit. I was flattered—overwhelmed, really—by Alexander's seduction, but worried as well, because the physical attraction wasn't mutual. And yet, swept up by his brilliance—the depth and breadth and height of the world Alexander seemed to move in—craving his wisdom, the magic he seemed to have at his fingertips and the illumination it promised, I made a private decision not to let this lack of sexual attraction stop me from having a romance with this amazing man. I'd let my libido determine my fate for long enough, I thought to myself. It was time to learn a new way to love.

I kissed Alexander's hand and held it tightly to my chest. That night, I stayed with him in the big white loft in Tribeca. It was Easter morning 1986.

FIVE

J UST WHEN I thought that life couldn't get any more out of control, Bob called from Los Angeles, asking me to come out and see him as soon as I could.

"There's something I need to tell you, darlin," he said in his familiar Texan drawl. "I don't want to do it on the phone." The pleading tone in Bob's voice told me that something bad was coming. I booked a flight to L.A. for the following week.

On the plane, I thought about the night that Bob and I met. I was seventeen, drunk as usual, waiting in the shadows of the only gay bar in Palm Springs for someone to pick me up. Through my stupor, I remember noticing a strange-looking man staring at me intensely across the pool table. He was wearing a ski cap on his head, with curly hair cascading down to his shoulders, like Wild Bill Hickok, mustache, plaid shirt unbuttoned nearly to the waist, and Levi's that looked as if they'd been spray painted onto his beautifully shaped rear end. Around his neck he wore something black, gnarled, and vaguely occult hanging from a chain.

"What's that?" I asked when he crossed the room and offered me a drink.

"A raven's claw," the guy said.

"Creepy."

He gave me a crinkle-eyed smile. "It helps me get what I want."

The next thing I knew, Bob and I were in his car, driving on the highway past Twentynine Palms to a turnoff at the Morongo Indian reservation. The fresh air sobered me enough to duck under the barbed wire fence and set out across the desert with this stranger. The moon was full and bright. Hot winds blew tumble-weed across the sand.

At dawn, after a night of sex, I woke up just as Bob was covering me with his jacket. The unexpected tenderness of this gesture from a man old enough to be my father touched me. When Bob asked me to move in with him three days later, I jumped at the chance to get out of Ida's house.

In addition to being my lover, Bob became my hero and mentor. He was in show business, a successful personal manager who specialized in finding lost boys—John Travolta, Patrick Swayze, Mickey Rourke were among his success stories—and turning them into leading men. Over the next five years, as we lived together, he worked his Pygmalion magic on me as well, grooming me and teaching me how to operate successfully in the world. He got me off booze and drugs, told me I was a writer, encouraged me to leave City College for Berkeley, and crowed like a proud father when I made Phi Beta Kappa. Bob showed me how to order champagne at the Excelsior in Florence; how to say "Excuse me?" instead of "Huh?"; got me into the movies as a dance extra in *Saturday Night Fever*. He gave me a glamorous life of Learjets and limousines, but in time I came to realize that it was not really *my* life, and though I was grateful to Bob for picking me up off the street, convincing me that I could be *somebody*, I struggled against his authority, too. Eventually this friction forced me to leave him, but Bob and I had managed to hold on to what was best between us—not friendship exactly, but a family bond too strong to ever be broken.

*

When I arrived at Bob's posh bungalow in Hancock Park, his houseboy, Steve, let me in and ushered me to a sofa in the living room. The stage for my arrival had been carefully set, the room lit only by candles. "He's nervous about seeing you," Steve told me.

"Is it bad?"

"Depends on the day. Today, yeah, pretty bad."

"I heard that, you little gossips!" Bob shouted from down the hall. Then he shuffled into the room in a knee-length T-shirt, hand-painted with skeletons and skulls, and a baseball cap pulled down low over his forehead.

"How do you like it?" he asked, holding the hem of his macabre costume and twirling around like Doris Day.

"You are the sickest person I've ever met." My remark fell flat. Sarcasm couldn't cover my shock at Bob's appearance. In spite of the low lighting, the loose clothing, the hat, Bob couldn't hide the fact that in the year since I'd seen him, he'd wasted to a scare-crow.

I tried to smile. Bob held out his arms. "Get over here and give me a hug!" he said. The sharpness of his shoulder blades cut against my palms.

I didn't know what to say. Luckily, Bob kept chattering. "I'm skinny, darlin', but I had the best skin on the ward. The nurses wouldn't leave me alone. They said they'd never seen a sick person *glow* before. You have no idea how I cheered that place up! When Travolta showed up I thought the nurses would drop a load. Needless to say, I was very, very popular."

"When aren't you?"

"You're right." Bob laughed. "I'm a light in the world." We sat on the sofa, and when Steve had left the room, Bob turned to me and began his prepared speech. "You know, darlin.'"

"I know, Bob."

"Stop that!" he insisted. Sick or not, Bob was still the most controlling person I'd ever met. "I want to tell you myself."

"Okay."

Bob took both my hands. "You know, I'm real sick and I'm not fixin' to get any better." He said this matter-of-factly, without self-pity. There was something else in his voice as well, which sounded almost like relief.

I said nothing. For a split second, I wondered whether Bob had given me this virus in the years before we knew it was spreading.

"Have you been tested?" he asked, picking up my thought.

"Not yet," I said, trying to sound casual. "I don't see the point."

"That's dumb."

"What am I supposed to do with the information?"

"Change your life," Bob answered. "You don't exactly look happy, you know."

"Please don't start."

"Do you really think you're doing what you were put here to do?"

"I love talking to Phoebe Cates about her hair. I live for it."

"Don't bullshit me. How do you feel?"

"Okay."

"You're thin."

"I'm always thin. I work eighty hours a week. I live on Chinese."

"No, honey. You're gaunt," he said. Bob couldn't help but nag me; I couldn't help but fight him. This was our way. But underneath the locking horns, there was love. After all these years, Bob was still trying to save my life.

*

When we first met, it was a life that needed saving. *Bad.* I was out of control, running wild in the streets, scrambling to get high any way I could—snorting, smoking, popping whatever I could get my hands on—*anything* to escape the claustrophobia of my mother's house. I was far too desperate to think about the future. Cheap thrills were easier—starting with sex.

It began when I was twelve. After Brian had died and Johnny had left her, my sister Joyce became a premiere fag hag, hanging out at the notorious Gold Cup coffee shop on Hollywood Boulevard—a famous brasserie for hustlers, drag queens, and low-life lechers. Sometimes, Joyce brought me along with her, thinking that her cute chicken brother would make her more popular with the boys.

One day, she introduced me to two of her new friends, an older guy named Jerry, who tickled the palm of my hand when he shook it, and his hot young blond lover, Mark, who winked at me when Joyce wasn't looking. The four of us instantly became a crowd. Joyce already had a mad crush on Mark, who made his living starring in porno flicks (his screen name was Mickey Palomino, "for obvious reasons," he bragged), while Jerry, an unctuous fifty-year-old with a belly popping out of his shirt and a ducktail dripping with Brylcreem, fell hopelessly in love with me.

One afternoon when Joyce and Mark were swimming in the pool next door, Jerry sat me down at our kitchen table and fidgeted.

"What's up?" I asked.

"You know, you're a good kid."

"So?" I said.

"So there's something I wanna tell you." Jerry swallowed hard. "You probably don't know it yet, but you're a homosexual."

The word sounded strange coming out of his mouth. Even though I'd been fooling around with boys (and girls) for as long as I could remember, even though most of my after-school hours were spent playing proctologist with Rudy Filipacchi or diddling Ross Goldstein's boner in the alley behind the building, I'd never attached a label to this behavior, and certainly not one as conclusive and clinical as *homosexual*.

Jerry stared at me across the table with bloodshot eyes. "You get what I mean, kid?"

" 'Course," I said, trying to cover up my surprise. "I'm not dumb."

A week later when Jerry and Mark invited me to go with them to the beach, I figured I had nothing to lose. The three of us spent the day at the queer beach in Santa Monica. I lay on the towel between Jerry and Mark listening to *Suite Judy Blue Eyes* on the tape deck, sniffing their suntan lotion, waiting for them to make their move.

At the end of the day, we went to a nearby motel. While Jerry was in the shower, Mark stripped off his bathing suit and started parading his huge professional namesake around till I was squirming. Finally, he came over to where I was sitting, knelt down, and slowly kissed me. When Jerry emerged from the bathroom, the three of us got into bed and, for the next several hours, I lay there in ecstasy as these grown-up men took turns going down on me. Staring up at the fan turning round and round on the ceiling, I felt like a prince being served by his first harem.

This episode opened the door to grown-up sex. I learned fast that I could get what I wanted with my body, that my cock could be a source of power, that I could manipulate people's behavior toward me—and, in so doing, the movements of my own fate—by manipulating my hips.

The outcast feelings I'd known as a boy, the fear that any minute I would be abandoned or forgotten, were swept aside by the discovery that as long as I could make people want me, I wouldn't get hurt. More than that, I learned that as long as I could entice them with the prospect of getting me in the sack, dangling myself like a carrot in front of their noses, I could get the attention I craved (and get off in the process).

Sex became a game: all I had to do was walk to a curb and stick my thumb out and, nine times out of ten, a gay man would pick me up and make me a proposition. At first, I was easy and let them do me in exchange for the ride—usually to Hollywood Boulevard and the Gold Cup where I spent most afternoons, sitting at the counter, thriving on the attention. As time went on and I got slicker, I learned to suss these guys out for what else they might have to offer: a swim in the pool at their mansion, a bag of pot, an invitation to a private party at the Beverly Hills Hotel. Sex gained me entrée to the wide spectrum of gay life, from posh to sleaze, and though I would have liked to have been appreciated for my brains and personality, I knew that, at thirteen and a half, this was unlikely. I also knew, instinctively, that this exposure to the big world, away from the dark swamp of my mother's house, would somehow save my life. If I had to fuck to get there, I was ready to do it.

Like anyone learning to work a new angle, I made mistakes, found myself trapped in ugly, dangerous situations with people I was ashamed to know, and from which I could not always extricate myself. First I fell in with a joker named Harold—a three-hundred-pound former Hell's Angel, who made his living as the head of a child pornography ring and wanted to keep me for his number-one boy, but balked when I refused to do anything in front of a camera.

A short time later, I spent six weeks riding around Palm Springs in the back of a limousine, having liquid LSD dripped in my eyeball while the crowd of tennis-playing rich kids who'd picked me up on Santa Monica Boulevard ran their bizarre games, culminating one night—in a scene reminiscent of *Satyricon*—with a double-jointed, seventy-year-old coke hag named Daisy being held up, naked and bone-thin, her ankles tucked behind her neck, and passed around the room like a plucked chicken.

I spent a few months as the mascot to a group of black drag queens who shot smack and took me out to the clubs with them at night, wrapped in their antique shawls, with gardenias in their hair in homage to Billie Holiday. Unfortunately, the star of the group fell for me and, when I wouldn't pledge undying devotion, tried to pull off a double suicide by locking me in a room with him and setting it on fire. Luckily he was too stoned to stop me from crawling out the window, and I never saw him again.

These adventures taught me a lot about the promises and pitfalls of sex—but not quite enough. There was something more I wanted to prove about what my body was worth—not in favors, but in cold hard cash. Hustling was the logical next step, but I wasn't sure how to go about it. Shameless as I was, the thought of standing on Las Palmas Avenue with the homeless, alleycat boys seemed beneath me. On the other hand, a callboy service seemed too tame, defeating my primary fantasy: to be purchased ON SIGHT. I wanted to haggle over dollars and cents with someone desperate to get in my pants; to toy with them, to raise the price, toy some more, and finally, in my own good time, take them for a pretty penny.

The right moment presented itself on a trip to San Francisco when I was fourteen. A guy I met at Harold's house sent me a round-trip ticket to visit him, and one afternoon while he was at work, I took a bus to Market Street, where I'd seen hookers on the corner through the window of his Jag.

The street was deserted when I got there—it was too early in the day, I guessed, but I was determined to try anyway. I sat on a fire hydrant in my bellbottom jeans and lit up a cigarette, imitating the loose-slung, available-but-contemptuous mock aloofness I'd seen the guys on Las Palmas use, following the eyes of drivers as they passed, sucking on my cigarette, turning away, blowing smoke rings. Every now and then, when I knew that someone was really looking, I let my hand fall casually to my basket and gave it a squeeze.

I saw the john before he saw me, lingering outside the bank across the street, and stared in his direction until our eyes met. He was white-haired, middle-aged, respectable in a three-piece suit and, as he gazed back at me, I felt my hook sinking into his skull. I held him with a smile, then reeled him in. The guy crossed the street, pretending to be casual, and made his way along the sidewalk to where I was sitting. He looked like Walter Cronkite.

"Watcha up to?" he asked, visibly nervous to be talking to me, glancing this way and that to make sure that no one he knew was watching.

"What do you think?"

He looked me up and down, fast, and asked, "How much?"

"Fifty bucks."

"You're kidding." The guy chuckled and rocked back and forth on his heels. "That's a lot of money, kid."

"I'm a lot of man," I said.

We got into the guy's car and went to a motel on Folsom Street. He asked me to duck when we pulled into the parking lot and, after he got the key, we walked separately to the room.

When we got there, he said he wanted to fuck me.

"I don't think so," I said. I'd been on the bottom a couple of times with Rudy and I liked it, but in terms of self-image, I preferred to be on top.

The guy was persistent. "For fifty dollars, I want some pussy," he said.

"Do I look like a pussy to you?"

He ran his finger down the V of my shirt till my nipples were showing. "You sure could."

I thought fast. "That'll cost you twenty more."

"I think I can handle that," he said, taking off his shiny black shoes, slipping them neatly beneath the bed.

"Let me see it," I said, remembering a TV show I'd seen where the hooker made the guy show her the cash before she got undressed.

The guy pulled his wallet from his back pocket and fanned the billfold open. It was full of twenties. He was obviously rich and looked clean. His nails were manicured. "Okay," I said, "but make it quick."

I took off my clothes and got down on my knees at the edge of the bed. The guy took off his suit pants but not his shirt, tie, or knee-high black socks. He rolled up his sleeves and tied the bottom of his shirt up over his belly, like Annette Funicello. Then he pulled his blue boxer shorts down around his knees and started yanking on himself while I waited.

When he was finished, the guy took his wallet with him into the bathroom and, when he came out in a towel a few minutes later, gripped it between his teeth. "You can pay me now," I said.

He chuckled, the way he had when I'd quoted my price on the street. "Greedy little kid, aren't you?" he said.

"I want my money."

"You'll *get* your money. When I decide to give it to you."

Unless I wanted to roll him, which was a bad idea, since he out-weighed me by seventy-five pounds, I was at his mercy and waited impatiently as we left the room and drove back to Market Street, stone silent, like strangers in an elevator waiting for the door to open. At the curb where he'd found me, the guy pulled a wad of bills out of his pocket and handed it to me. "Good pussy," he said to me.

I jumped out of the car and slammed the door as hard as I could. He sped away before I could count the money—eight singles wrapped in a twenty.

That's what I'm worth, I thought.

A few years later I met Bob and he convinced me that this wasn't true. I could be a player, he said, if only I learned to clean up my act and stop selling myself so cheap.

The morning after I arrived in Los Angeles, lying side by side on his bed, I asked Bob how he really felt now that he was sick. He was wearing an electric blue kimono, holding his hands over his chest, doing some form of Oriental self-healing.

"You want to know the truth?" he replied, moving his palms down to his belly.

"Yeah."

"I've never been happier in my life."

At first I thought that Bob was being sarcastic, then I realized he wasn't. The fact was that even though he was fading fast, Bob seemed extremely peaceful—content to be at home, retired from show biz, free of the relentless demands of his infantile clients. He was more down to earth than I'd ever known him to be, with time to pursue his quieter interests. That morning he'd played the piano for me—Satie's "Gymnopaedie," a piece he hadn't touched in twenty years.

There was something else as well. From the pile of books next to his bed—with titles like *A Gradual Awakening, Who Dies?* and *Meetings at the Edge*—I deduced that Bob's literary tastes had shifted from Judith Krantz to spirituality.

"Tell me the truth," I teased him. "Have you found God?"

"You mean has God found *me*. Stephen thinks so."

"Stephen?"

"Levine, the guy who wrote those books. He says that—how does it go?—'the thing we're looking for is the thing that's looking.'"

"I like that."

"We have these talks when I freak out. He tells me dying isn't the end."

"Oh, really?"

"On the other hand, I tell him who *cares* if it's not the end if *I'm* not gonna be there?"

"That's supposed to be the good news, I think."

"Well, I don't like it. I'm gonna miss *me*. And you wanna know what else?"

"Tell me."

Bob turned to me, dead serious. "I'll miss shopping."

On the morning I was packing to leave, Bob was sprawled out on the sofa, telling me what to fold first. "Do you think I've changed?" he asked.

"You're still the bossiest person I know."

"And you're the stubbornest. *Don't* do your underwear first. Use them for packing when you're finished."

I did as Bob instructed.

"No," he said. "I mean, have I changed *inside*?"

"You do seem different," I admitted. Bob was so much softer now.

"I'm trying," he said. "I really am."

"It shows."

Bob smiled. Then he said, "You know this maniac you're seeing?"

"Alexander?" Bob had listened to me the night before, describing my new favorite person for hours.

"Right. Well, he sounds like he can teach you something. Like Stephen."

"I think he can."

"I sure wish I'd met someone like that when I was your age." This was a strange thing for Bob to say. He never regretted anything.

"Maybe I'll be able to give you something for a change," I said, putting in my underwear last, and zipping up the suitcase.

"*Thank* you," he said, rolling his eyes.

When Bob walked me to the door, we hugged for a long time. I kissed him and saw that his eyes were wet.

"Cut it out," I said. "I'll be back. I'll see you soon."

"Right," he said, looking away.

I grabbed him hard, again, and walked out quickly to the waiting cab.

SIX

T HE VIRUS SEEMED to be everywhere now. Soon after I returned from seeing Bob in Los Angeles, John pulled up the sleeve of his shirt to show me three new lesions that had appeared that week, running like bruises up and down his arm. It was six months since our trip to Jamaica.

"They're coming fast," he said, looking tousled and confused, like a little boy.

"I'm sure I've got it too," I answered.

"Is that supposed to make me feel better?"

I didn't know what else to say. The truth was that as John got sicker, I felt secretly more fortunate. If Aristotle was right in defining luck as the moment the arrow hits the guy next to you, then I was indeed a lucky man, sitting there while John was falling. But my luck was mixed with grief and guilt, and the constant awareness that, but for a spin of the wheel, a tilt of the stars, it could have been me with those lesions, with someone luckier looking on.

People died so quickly then. The doctors killed them, meaning well, with drugs they hadn't yet learned to use. John was one of the guinea pigs sacrificed in trial and error.

Later that summer he was admitted to Roosevelt Hospital with a relatively mild case of Pneumocystis carinii, a condition for which he would now be treated and released in two weeks, with a prognosis of good health for years to come. Instead on that August day in 1986, John was quarantined behind a door plastered with dire warnings, and overdosed with a battery of chemicals that turned him in a week from a sick man to a dying man, ten pounds thinner, with legs like sticks.

We didn't know what else to do. We didn't know then about asking questions, refusing treatment. At the time, there was nowhere to turn but to the drugs, and John went down like a straw man.

He swallowed the pills; he puked them up.

They put him on IVs; his skin turned chalky.

"I'm trapped," he said, when I asked him how he felt.

"In the hospital?"

"In my body."

Two weeks passed.

One Tuesday evening I arrived at the hospital with takeout food for both of us. John had had a terrible day of painful tests and high fevers. When I entered the room, he was flat on his back with an oxygen mask over his face, watching football on the TV suspended from the ceiling. His eyes were open wide and he was panting fast, like a dog, twisting the bedsheet between his fists. When I pulled it up to cover him, he pushed it back down to his hips. He looked panicked.

"Rough day, huh?" I asked. He nodded, his eyes still fixed on the TV screen.

Pushing the damp blond hair from his forehead, I sat by the bed and watched the dent in the center of his chest rising and falling. His eyes followed the neon jerseys scrambling and falling across the screen.

The hospital hygiene was appalling, trash cans overflowing with dirty tissues ignored by nurses too scared to touch them, even through plastic gloves. When I repeatedly told them that this mess was unacceptable, they shrugged and told me to empty the garbage myself. I was ashamed putting the gloves on—I refused to wear the mask they recommended—ashamed that even though I was probably infected, I was still scared to be in that room. When John coughed, I jumped involuntarily. I kissed him on the cheek, teeth locked, and wiped my lips when he turned away.

Had I known that it was his last night, I would have stayed. Instead, around eleven, I said good night and asked if there was anything he wanted before I left.

"Gum," John said, through the oxygen mask. I left the room in search of a vending machine. I ran up and down the hall plastered with warning signs, faces peering out at me through doors ajar—big eyes, wispy hair—grown men curled like babies alone in half-dark rooms.

When I returned with a pack of Wrigley's, John pulled the mask aside and opened his mouth. I put the gum on his cakey tongue and he smiled, as sweetly as a little boy. Five hours later John died.

It all happened too quickly to comprehend—the call in the morning; the funeral and service; Schwartzkopf singing *The Four Last Songs*. Helping to empty John's apartment that weekend, I felt numb, moving automatically through the shelves full of opera records, the Armani suits and expensive ties, the kitchenware he never used, the dog-eared pile of takeout menus, still not fully believing that he was gone. In my mind, John seemed to be merely out of the room; any minute, I expected him to come loping in—gawky, sweet, with his Walkman clipped to his shorts—and we'd go downstairs to sit on the stoop, watch the boys, and kvetch. We'd get a bite at the Empire Diner and, afterward, go our separate ways, knowing that whatever happened, the two of us would be there again next week and the week after that.

The fist in my gut was getting tighter. Life at *Interview* went from maddening to intolerable. With matters of life or death closing in around me, the demands of the magazine seemed more ridiculous than ever. My pleasure at scooping my colleagues, bagging the big name and dropping it at Doris's feet like a drooling retriever, was gone for good. Let Kim Basinger give her cover to *Vanity Fair*, or walk off the end of the Brooklyn Bridge—it all felt the same to me.

Sensing my growing apathy, Alexander stepped up his efforts to inspire me with daily dharma packages, like a spiritual cheer-leader. I appreciated his intentions, but the gap between the life I was leading and the one I wanted was too glaring for his pep talks to heal.

Finally, walking arm in arm on the beach at Southampton one late afternoon two weeks after John died, Alexander popped the question.

"What do you think your chances are of being alive in five years?" he asked.

Without thinking, I answered, "Fifty-fifty." My pessimism, and the certainty with which I'd said this, surprised us both. Alexander stopped and took both of my hands in his. There were seagulls in the air behind him; his hair was matted, his eyes gentle.

"Then come with me to India," he said. He pulled an airline ticket out of his pocket. "This is first class," he said. "They're sending me to Burma to write about the temples of Pagan. I can trade it in for two coach tickets."

"I can't accept that."

"Listen," he said, gripping my shoulders. "I'm trying to help you save your own life. Don't you understand that?"

"I don't understand anything."

"Well, at least try to understand this. You will never have this chance again."

I knew in my heart that he was right.

"Tell me the truth. Do you want your life to mean something? Do you want your spirit healed?"

I stared at the sand; no words could express how desperately I did. But I secretly feared that it was too late. John had died so quickly.

"Do you really *want* to be alive in five years, Mark?"

"Yes," I said. "Of course I do."

"Then let go of your pride and trust me. You don't know where this way leads, but you know the other way inside and out, and it will take you nowhere. You must take a chance while you have it. You must try *not* knowing for a change. This journey might soften your heart and, God willing, your head."

"That's what I'm afraid of."

"It's the best thing that could happen to you. I pray with every atom of my being to see you lose your mind and turn into a blissful idiot."

"Terrific."

Then Alexander danced in the sand, arms akimbo, and threw back his head, roaring with laughter.

That night I had the first visionary experience of my life. Although it occurred while I was sleeping, it was not a dream. The texture, clarity, and effect were entirely different. I recorded it in my journal:

Alexander and I fell asleep after talking about our plans for India. Almost immediately, I find myself in a stone room, with crude cutout windows and doors, approximately twenty feet square. The room is on the top of a mountain—outside, a sheer drop of green hills embedded with stones. There are two rows of six chairs each at the center of the room facing each other, and a dozen other people present whose faces I don't focus on.

We sit in the chairs. Alexander is opposite me, looking at me intensely. Behind him is a small bald man in a brick-colored cassock, who leads the people from their seats one by one. I know without being told that he is a holy man. When my turn comes, the man takes me from my chair and removes my clothes. He starts to work with my body, twisting and touching me, in preparation for some ritual. He slips a robe of fine, tattered cloth like his, only lighter in color, over my shoulders, and a skullcap on my head. I am barefoot. Then he bends at the knees, lifts me onto his shoulders, and starts to spin, slowly at first, then faster and faster until the room is a blur. Hanging high in the corner of the room is a triangular cone of fluorescent light approximately two feet long— bright, white, crackling. The holy man spins me over to the corner, and when we enter its field, I'm filled with a strange, buzzing energy. Suddenly the man becomes a woman with a fierce face. She growls at me in some unknown language and a voice in me growls back in the same language, without moving my lips. Then he-she bends at the knees, pops up, and throws me up from his shoulders into the triangle. When I hit it, I *pop* like a bug in a lamp.

In that second, I opened my eyes and sat straight up in bed, my body tingling, feeling strange and exhilarated.

"What is it?" Alexander asked.

I told him exactly what had happened. He smiled.

"That was an initiation," he said, pulling me down on the bed beside him. "Be grateful."

When I gave my resignation at the office, colleagues were shocked and envious. Doris, never inclined to generosity of spirit, made a honking noise as if I'd volunteered to skydive off the Triboro Bridge. She told me I was making a big mistake. "They'll forget you in two weeks," she said, meaning the gods of magazine publishing.

"I don't really care."

"So what are you gonna do, become a Hindu?" she asked with contempt.

"I need to recharge my batteries," was all I said, knowing that any effort to communicate my real distress would be entirely wasted.

"Well just don't eat anything you can't peel," Doris said, turning back to page six of the *Post*. Two weeks later, when I went upstairs to say good-bye, in lieu of a gold watch, a send-off party, a hug perhaps to thank me for saving her ass a thousand times, Doris told me to take some petty cash and buy myself a pizza.

Andy was even less generous. He leered when he passed my office and, as if to insult me, sent an assistant to remove me from the building late one night. I demanded an explanation. The assistant came back with an embarrassed look. "He doesn't want you stealing anything," he said.

My friends pretended to understand what I was doing and why, but only my buddy, James—an actor on his own quest for self-discovery—really did. The others called me dramatic, accused me of exaggeration, or insisted, as Carole had, that what I called an abyss was really a passing slump, that if only I'd get myself a prescription for antidepressants, or redo my apartment, or buy some clothes, I would be myself again. They couldn't understand why in the world I'd give up my job when I was ripe to be hired away by an even better magazine, why I would travel to a Third World country with a (possibly) compromised immune system, why I would give up my lease. Or they humored me, thinking that I had been swept away by this brilliant English poet, missing the point and the seriousness of my intent.

On August 11, a few days before leaving New York, I had another bizarre dream. In it, I was holding a flat, shiny bronze tablet shaped like the slab that Charlton Heston carried down the mountain in *The Ten Commandments*. The tablet was divided into six squares, five of which contained symbols—clover, acorn, sword, and so forth—that I "knew" corresponded to people I had loved who had died. The last square was empty, reserved, I suspected in the dream, for me.

I was wrong. The next morning, Steve called from California to say that Bob had died painlessly in his sleep at 3 A.M. the night before.

Alexander sent me a note that read:

> *This journey will be difficult—make no mistake—the tests are* grueling *and you will undoubtedly be tempted to turn back many times. But remember: In order to answer the questions that are haunting you now, you must explore a dimension about which you know nothing. Try not to forget the essential point that on the other side of this confusion, which will keep you in its throes for years, is an existence you cannot begin to imagine, blessed by love and freedom from every fear. You will have to be strong in order to break through, but believe me, my darling, there is no other choice worth making."*

My last night in New York, my three closest friends, Carole,

Robert, James, and I had our last supper. It was an emotional meeting for all of us, not knowing when we would meet again, how long I'd be gone, who might die in the meantime. The scent of finality and fate was in the air as we toasted one another.

"Don't forget us," said Carole. My imminent departure was hardest on her.

"I'll be back to haunt you," I said.

"Speaking of haunting, what about a will?" Robert, my ex-lover and self-appointed older brother, was both logical and cautious.

"What am I gonna leave? My underwear?" I asked.

"It doesn't matter, everybody needs a will." Robert forced me to sit at the typewriter and compose an informal last testament, scattering the few belongings I owned among my friends and family. I signed the document, sealed it in an envelope, and gave it to Robert as my executor.

Later, after we'd all had a good cry, the four of us stood in a circle, hugging by the door.

Afterwards, James and I walked to the subway together. At the top of the stairs he handed me a slip of paper, then kissed me and crossed to the downtown platform. I unfolded the paper and found this message: "Every journey has a secret destination of which the traveler is unaware," he said, quoting Martin Buber. "Be careful."

PART TWO
OUT OF MY MIND

SEVEN

ALEXANDER HAD A surprise for me. Shortly after my arrival in Paris, he informed me that we would be stopping en route to India to visit a woman he knew in Germany.

"Who is she?" I asked.

"The less you know, the better," he said.

It's a testament to how completely I'd put myself in Alexander's hands that I let it rest at that.

In the meantime, Alexander showed me his odd Parisian life, which surpassed in Proustian detail the one he had described in his novel. There was the miniscule jewel-box flat in Saint-Sulpice, filled with Russian icons, Hindu sculpture, incense, and clutter; nightly dinners with millionaires and baronesses (once, when the buzzer rang, he actually said, "Oh shit, it's the empress of the Holy Roman Empire," and it was); long, slow walks across the Seine to the haunted Place Georges Cain; drunken dinners at the Cafetière; visits to the Indian collection at the Musée Guillemet; strolls through the Tuileries to watch the queers weave in and out of bushes in various states of undress.

I was impressed, and slightly confused, by Alexander's mixture of mysticism and worldliness. When I asked him how he could be so wild *and* on a spiritual path he reminded me not to be fooled by appearances. He assured me that the sacred and profane are all the same in the eyes of God, that it is all part of the same feast. Hungry to absorb what I could of this new outlook, overjoyed to be free of my life in New York, I took Alexander at his word, and was swept along by the whirlwind of his passion with absolutely no idea what would happen next.

We took a train to Frankfurt and arrived at twilight in the nondescript village of Thalheim, dominated by a church steeple just like a thousand others in the German countryside. Herbert, the huge, bespectacled man who met us at the train station, drove us to a modest house overgrown with vines and warned us not to talk as we entered. *Darshan*, whatever that was, had already begun.

The Baal Shem Tov, a Hasidic master who lived two hundred years ago in Poland, once compared the moment of his awakening to turning and stepping out the back door of his own mind. At 7:30 P.M. on August 24, 1986, I stepped through the back door of my own. With absolutely no preparation, I was shaken to the core, changed— in seconds—from a man who thought he knew the world to a man aware that he knew nothing.

As I crossed the threshold into the foyer, my ears began to ring. I rubbed them hard to make the sound stop, but the buzzing continued, like a swarm of bees or static on the radio, breaking the room's otherwise eerie quiet. I looked at Alexander, who pointed to his own ears and nodded his head, indicating that I should follow him up the stairs.

Then I saw her. Peeking over the top of the banister, my eyes fell on a tiny Indian woman in a vermilion sari, sitting on a chair, her eyes closed, holding the head of a kneeling child between her fingers. Her dark face was serene—her shoulders slightly hunched as she touched the boy's temples, the two of them frozen in a strange tableau as he held her feet. Neither of them moved at all as I watched.

Finally, the woman opened her eyes, released his head, and sat back, gazing straight into the boy's eyes. Her expression was fierce and unwavering, her head rocking slightly forward as she examined him another minute, until finally she lowered her eyes and gazed down at her hands. The boy touched his forehead to the ground and returned to his chair, making way for an old woman, who hobbled to the carpet and knelt with difficulty, the whole process beginning again.

I was mesmerized by the sight of her. I knew immediately, without knowing *how* I knew, that this woman was unlike any human being I'd seen before—qualitatively different—as if she belonged to another species. I recognized viscerally, not logically, as one would recognize a taste or a smell, that she was something other. Her stillness, her silence, the curve of her shoulders in silhouette, or more than that, the atmosphere that surrounded her, reminded me of something enormous and ancient, like a mountain.

I sat on the stairs and closed my eyes. Immediately, the background of my inner vision turned golden orange and I felt myself sinking into a kind of trance, my body heavy, my head light. Against this glowing background, the woman appeared, flying in slow motion, taking me up with her, bouncing me through space like a seal with a ball. I was aware that I was somewhere outside myself, observing from an odd remove as she soared back and forth, teasing me, pulling me further and further from my ordinary mind.

Alexander touched my shoulder. I opened my eyes and saw her sitting alone. It was my turn—she was waiting for me—I wanted to run in the opposite direction. Alexander tugged at my arm; finally I stood up and walked to the carpet in front of her. Feeling awkward and vaguely ridiculous, I knelt and lowered my head. I felt her fingers on my temples, her thumbs locking onto my head on either side of my fontanelle, finding their place and gripping like a vise. Touching her feet through the silk of her sari—they were cold and small, like a child's—I stared at the lines of gold in her hem. Strangely, other than the embarrassment of putting my head into the hands of someone I had never seen before and bowing in front of another person for the first time in my life, I felt nothing as I knelt there. I tried not to breathe too loudly and counted the seconds until it was over.

Finally she released my head and I sat back on my heels, looking into her dark eyes. Her face was blank and expressionless. The pupils of her eyes—which nearly filled the entire oval, like a cat's—flicked back and forth as she stared at me, as if they were seeing through me. I had the sense that she was actually *doing* something as she stared, as steady as if she were boring through a wall. It took every ounce of my strength not to look away. Finally she lowered her eyes and I returned to my place on the stairs.

She waited a minute more. When no one came forward, she stood—bringing all of us automatically to our feet—and without raising her eyes from the floor, slowly climbed the stairs to the top of the house, followed by an older Indian woman who had been sitting at her side.

The house emptied in minutes. Alexander led me down a narrow staircase to the kitchen in the basement and told me to wait there. My head was spinning, and as soon as I was alone, I began to invent explanations for what had happened to me on the stairs. I was overanxious, tired, stressed. I was succumbing to Alexander's otherworldly influence. I had been swept up by the strangeness of the woman sitting there silently, holding people's head in her hands. Alexander interrupted my thoughts.

"Mother Meera will see you now," he said, smiling in the doorway. "Follow me."

We climbed the stairs to the room where the woman had been

sitting earlier. She was standing perfectly still—no more than five feet tall—her attendant by her side, a sweater covering her sari. She gazed modestly at the floor.

My mind went completely blank. The four of us stood in silence for several minutes. Finally Alexander came to my rescue. "Mark just escaped from New York, Mother," he said. "His friends are dying. He may be sick too. He doesn't know anything about God. He needs your help."

I tried to think of something to say, but in this woman's presence, words seemed somehow superfluous. I looked up, and at that moment, she flashed me a knowing smile, her face becoming radiant. Our eyes met for a second, and then she looked away.

"You are welcome in the Mother's house," the other woman, Adilakshmi, said in singsong English.

"Thank you," I whispered. Mother Meera looked at me once more, smiled gently, and nodded her head, as if to confirm that explanations were unnecessary. She muttered several foreign words in a strange, growling voice to Adilakshmi.

"Mother says you will sleep tonight!" she translated. Then they turned and disappeared up the stairs.

Alexander was right when he said that I knew nothing about God.

Nominally we were Jewish, but we were bad Jews, fallen Jews, assimilated Jews—indistinguishable, except for the occasional Yiddishism, from the goyim. What our Jewishness meant, in practical terms, is that we ate twice as much pork as our gentile friends, got extra days off from school, and decorated a Styrofoam Star of David at Christmastime instead of a tree.

At Passover, my pious Russian grandfather stood at the end of the table, rocking in his tallis and yarmulke, reciting prayers that no one understood, while we fidgeted. My mother sucked on a Pall Mall, flicking ashes onto the carpet.

"Enough, already, for Chrissakes, Dad," she'd interrupt when we got to the plagues. "Flies, locusts, cattle disease," she'd mutter, rolling her eyes as we dipped our pinkies into the Mani-schewitz and dripped it, scourge by scourge, onto my grandmother's good china.

God was a nonissue in suburbia, a myth no one cared about, like Bigfoot. When the thought of a Creator did happen to float across my consciousness when I was a boy, it was immediately countered by cynicism. "What kind of sick God would create such a world?" I asked. "What sad excuse for a God would live here?" Still, being inquisitive, I couldn't help but wonder sometimes about the source of things, beginning with me. Between the ages of five and ten, I spent most of my free time locked in the bathroom, sitting on the sink, staring at myself in the mirror, looking for answers. I would gaze into my eyes for hours on end asking: Who are you? What are you? Where did you come from? Why are you here? No matter how long I sat there waiting, though, I got no response to my questions or to the deeper mystery: what was watching me from inside my eyes, this spark that made me see in the first place.

When I was twelve and three-quarters, I did a crash course in Talmud to please my grandpa, and at my Bar Mitzvah six months later, recited half an hour of Hebrew I didn't understand. Afterward, I walked around the reception hall with an empty shoe box, collecting $25 checks. Except for weddings and funerals, it was the last time I ever set foot in a temple.

The night of my Bar Mitzvah, my mother took me out to Dino's Pizzeria for a private dinner—"Just the two of us," she said. It was the first time I could remember her leaving my sisters at home to be alone with me, and it seemed odd. My mother put on lipstick and got all dolled up the way she did for Willy, and walking from the T-bird into our favorite restaurant, took my arm like a girl out on a date.

Inside, we ordered sausage heros. My mother asked for a "screwdriver without the screw," meaning mostly vodka, lit a cigarette, and looked at me across the red checkered tablecloth, her eyes shadowed by candlelight.

"What's up?" I asked her.

"Nothing," she answered. "Can't a mother take her son out to dinner without something being wrong?" She said it coyly, gazing at me with the strangest mixture of pride and pleasure and something else I couldn't quite put my finger on.

Finally, after my mother had finished her drink, she asked, "How do you compare to the other boys at school?"

"What do you mean, compare?"

"Down there," she answered, looking at her lap.

I felt like she'd stuck her hands down my pants. "Why?" I asked.

"Because there's something you should know."

I wasn't sure I wanted to.

"Your father was *enormous*," she said, mouthing the syllables slowly. "In all my life, I never saw that much man. Till the last time we did it, it hurt me." The moist look in my mother's eyes was positively indecent.

I didn't respond—I was too confused, not only by this unsolicited piece of information, but by my mother's interest and the implication of her message. Although I had always been sexual, this was the first time I'd thought of my penis as something to be measured, something separate from me. This led me to another conclusion as well—that man was measured by his sex—and since no one had been around to teach me otherwise, I lit on this image of plundering, pillaging cocksman as an ideal to shoot for. After that, sex had become

my substitute for God, my "prayer gone awry." The fervor I chan-
neled into getting laid was like a seeker's passion for truth, driven
by the same desperate thirst for union. Instead of reaching for love,
unfortunately, the impulse was slightly twisted in me, trying to be
the kind of grandiose God my mother wanted, the kind my father
was—*enormous.*

When I arrived in Thalheim, that was all I knew about a higher
power. Except this: that if by some miracle I was ever to believe in
God, it would have to be on radically truthful terms. Under no cir-
cumstances would I be seduced by some kind of spiritual cover-up
that told me pretty lies, like I was blessed when I was sinning, safe
when so many I knew were dying, loved when there was so much
hatred everywhere. Dignity, in my view, meant facing the hard facts
of life with as little fantasy as possible. These hard facts would never
break me, I promised myself—God-hunger would never break me
either, even if I wanted more than anything else for such an entity to
exist. The possibility was almost too beautiful to imagine; so beautiful, in fact, that this longing became the knife that made the gash that
made the scream that made my life.

EIGHT

MY FIRST NIGHT in Thalheim, in a room directly under Mother Meera's quarters, I slept for fifteen hours.

It was a sleep unlike any I'd experienced before, dominated by vivid, clear dreams. Again, as in my trance on the stairs, Mother Meera appeared, flying around in various costumes, changing shape and color. Pink first, she gently stroked my head, tucked against her soft breast; next she was a demonic red, her eyes cruel, fangs protruding from her mouth, fingers tipped with claws like a bird of prey. Blood dripped from the corner of her mouth and she tore savagely at my belly with her talons, ripping at my entrails. I screamed and clutched my stomach, to protect myself, but I was powerless, and finally, exhausted, surrendered to her fury, floating limply in midair like a doll with its stuffing torn out.

When I woke, Alexander had his arms around me and I was sobbing. He rocked me while I cried for two hours, curled up in the blanket. A grief no therapist had come close to evoking had been unleashed; like a cyst that had been lanced, the hardness in my belly poured out its poisons in spasms. Afterward, I took the first easy breath I could remember taking in years, and the crying stopped as mysteriously as it had started. I felt as clean and light and fresh as a child.

*

That afternoon, Alexander and I went for a walk outside the village, along a deserted road past the cemetery and fields where sheep and cows were grazing, up into the woods behind Thalheim. The lightness that followed my morning ordeal had not passed. I felt wonderful.

"Why didn't you warn me?" I asked Alexander. "Who *is* she?"

Alexander told me Mother Meera's story: The daughter of farmers, she was born Kamala Reddy in the village of Chandepalle, Andhra Pradesh, India, on December 26, 1960. Her family was not especially religious and she was not raised in any tradition. Her relationship with her family was never close; her real parents were the spiritual guides she met in visions, and it was to them that she turned for the love and help she needed.

Her spiritual evolution was rapid and complete. She had no human guru, read no religious philosophy, did no *sadhana*, or spiritual practice: her contact with the absolute was immediate and unmediated. At six, she had her first experience of *samadhi*, falling senseless for a day—an experience, she says, that taught her the detachment from earthly desires that others can spend a lifetime learning.

Two years later, at age eight, she was sent to work in the home of Venkat Reddy (no relation). Reddy had been having visions of the Divine Mother since childhood and had sat at the feet of several holy women during his spiritual search. They had, however, left him unsatisfied. When his uncle died, Reddy was forced to return to his village to manage his property. There he was immediately struck by the power emanating from young Kamala and, living in her presence, was soon convinced that she was exceptional.

In Reddy's story of his first experience with Mother Meera's psychic abilities, she had gone to stay fifty miles away.

> I was lying on my bed one evening. I heard her voice calling me and was amazed. How could she come all that way? I got up and looked for her. I could not find her anywhere. Later, I went to the city where she was. She said to me, "I came to you and you did not notice anything. I called out to you and you didn't hear." I asked her how she had come that far. She just said that there was "another way of traveling."

When Mother Meera's extraordinary gifts became impossible to deny, Reddy left his family and business affairs to dedicate his life to protecting her. For the next several years, Mother Meera related her experience in other dimensions to Mr. Reddy. "She would often go into *samadhi* for fourteen hours without a break," wrote Reddy. "She would sleep and eat very little. Eventually, she would learn to be in a trance continually, which she is, with open eyes."

On our second afternoon, Alexander and I again walked up toward the woods behind Thalheim, along the muddy trail that bordered the pastures where black and white cows were grazing, past apple orchards and farmers in tractors, who nodded at us suspiciously, then turned back to their work, trying not to stare at the strange intruders in city clothes.

We walked across the field toward a stand of pine trees. As we approached, we stopped talking and, entering the grove, walked quietly, needles crackling under our feet, to a large stump, where we sat side by side to rest. It was an enchanted scene. The quiet sun was filtering down through the treetops in slants of light. I took Alexander's hand and we sat there, staring, listening to each other breathe, watching the moisture rise up off the ground, coloring the panes of light like smoke.

I stared into the grove for several minutes and then saw something so strange I could not believe my eyes. Mother Meera was standing thirty feet away, clear as day, twirling and dancing among the trees, trailing a pink, gauzelike fabric. My eyes were open; we had not been drinking or taking drugs; there was no sense of hallucination or even strangeness, just the figure of Mother Meera—about half the size she was in real life, but otherwise the same—turning and floating thirty feet away from where I sat. I blinked and watched, but before it could register fully, the apparition was gone.

Alexander believed in these visions. I did not and was becoming increasingly confused by what I'd seen since arriving in Thalheim.

"What *is* she?" I asked him, afterward, walking along the stream toward Dorndorf.

"What do you think she is?"

"I have no idea. I have nothing to compare her to."

"Mother is an enlightened being."

"What exactly do you mean by enlightened?"

"I mean that she is in direct contact at all times with God. I mean that she is fully conscious of, and operating at, many, many levels of reality at every moment. She is able to travel to other dimensions, to know what is in others' hearts, to see the soul with open eyes."

"How do you *know* this?"

"Because she has proven it to me time and time again. Can you explain what happened to you on the stairs? Or the sound in your ears? Your dreams or the vision you saw just now?"

I was forced to admit I couldn't.

"Of course you can't. All you can do is doubt. That's the ego's only defense against mystical reality: doubt, disclaim, deconstruct, destroy."

"You mean she's a guru?"

"In a sense," Alexander said, sitting on a bench overlooking the valley. "Guru means dark to light; anyone or anything that serves to enlighten is a guru. A book can be a guru, lightning can be a guru, a child can be a guru. In that sense, Mother is certainly a guru, a master, a teacher. But most human gurus work very hard for their own realization; they do practice, they follow and impose rules. Mother has no discipline per se. She offers no discourses or religion. She gives direct spiritual help to whoever needs it."

I knew what he meant—merely seeing Mother Meera had awakened something in me, a sense of recognition, clear and unspoken.

Alexander continued. "In a certain sense, enlightenment is a relative quality. One person may be more enlightened than another. But it is not a finite quantity—as in, 'Now I'm enlightened'—it is a process without end, with its own road signs and hazards. Follow?"

"I think so."

"There are different levels of enlightenment or attainment, some more unusual than others. There are thousands of Buddhist monks around the world but only one Dalai Lama. There were thousands of Hindu monks around the world, but only one Ramakrishna. There were a thousand Christians after Jesus, but only one Saint Francis. Think of light: it is everywhere, but concentrated more intensely in some places than in others. Enlightened beings are concentrated sources of light. Each has his or her own unique personality, but behind this mask of difference, their motive, purpose, and essence are identical."

"But isn't that true of all of us?"

"Strictly speaking, yes. Fundamentally, we are all, in essence, enlightened beings waiting to realize it. But the difference between an ordinary person and someone in that state of consciousness is quantum. It's like the difference between a reptile and a bird: they have a common origin, but the bird has grown wings."

"And what about Mother Meera?"

"She is a particularly rare case because she was born already conscious. These powers come naturally to her. She has said that she knew, before she entered a body, who and what she was. It is extremely rate, but it *can* happen that certain individuals are born enlightened. History is full of examples. Mother Meera is one."

"And what about the rest of us?"

"We have to walk barefoot over glass to get there. We have to beg and weep and pound our chests. The art of awakening is like any other art: the only way to master it is through practice. A soprano does her scales, an athlete runs every morning; nothing worthwhile—least of all the spiritual life—happens without work."

"You make it sound like hard labor."

"It is," he insisted, "but not in the sense that you mean. Because in spiritual life, every step is also a joy and brings new strength, a deepening and broadening of the mind and heart. You are encouraged along the way by vision and bliss. You take one step toward God and God takes two steps toward you."

"And a teacher is necessary for this?"

"Absolutely. If you want to learn Greek, you've got to have a professor. You have to meet someone who is already enlightened to show you that such a state is possible. Occasionally," Alexander continued, "some other kind of shattering experience, illness or sudden grief, can blow the mind off its hinges and reveal the light of God. But for most of us, the first glimmerings of this enlightened consciousness come through contact with holy beings. That is how it happened for me with Mother.

"This contact is crucial. When you watch someone operating from a position of absolute love, something in your soul responds. Enlightenment is the natural destiny of human beings, the reason we're here, the missing link between chaos and order. Without understanding this, people understand nothing. Life is a meaningless series of births and deaths and excruciating pain without redemption."

"Part of me still believes it is."

"Of course you do. And you will continue to in some part of yourself for the rest of your life. You must be *dead honest* about this. Never pretend to be further along than you are. Spiritual hypocrisy is the worst hypocrisy, and your authentic doubt is your best friend, provided you understand that it is there to help you toward the light."

Alexander continued, without pausing for me respond.

"Think about love," he said. "We use that word to mean everything it isn't, but what is love truly? It is action in alignment with nature, nature attuned to the force pulsing through your veins and the veins of the planet. People who are in that dimension of love are in God. They are illumined. Think of it as a form of genius. Everyone has a touch of it, but some have concentrated and harnessed it to the point where it bears fruit and spreads something wonderful in the world."

"So Mother Meera is a spiritual genius?"

"Of the highest kind. People like Mother are here, in a body, showing us that enlightenment is ordinary, tangible, that we are *not* the end of human evolution but merely a stage of it—thank God. I think that's why most people are so depressed. They think that this is the end of the line, that nothing is ever really going to change in the human condition. But the enlightened masters like Mother tell us not to worry too much about the bigger picture until we've actually perfected ourselves. It's better to keep it simple and keep your eye turned inward until it can see—and is softened enough to view the situation out there with the utmost compassion. If you observe Mother carefully, you'll see how gently she does everything; she never tells anyone what to do. The strongest are the most gentle."

"And the most silent."

"That's how it's always been. The wisest speak the least, and when they do, they speak in a few, well-chosen words, in simple speech, in parable. Unlike me!"

We had reached the top of the ridge and sat quietly for a long time on a bench overlooking Thalheim. "It's beginning to make sense," I said. "But I don't want to worship anyone."

"Don't worship, then. It's not your path. Scrutinize. But keep your eyes open and admit the truth of what you see."

Walking through the woods above Thalheim, I made a pact with myself: to believe nothing without experience, take nothing second-hand. I intended to observe, understand, and deduce for myself; to make use of all my powers of doubt and discrimination. Much as Alexander impressed me, I would not be seduced by his predisposition to faith. Driven by the fear of losing my mind and credibility, of becoming some kind of Shirley MacLaine woo-woo or God-I'm-gonna-die convert, I decided to err in the opposite direction: to keep my hard head, draw no conclusions, and wait.

In the days that followed, I watched Mother Meera like a hawk, waiting for some misstep, some indication that she was not the enlightened being Alexander claimed she was. But I could find no evidence that she was a fake. Whether giving *darshan* or walking to the bank, she was the same—self-contained, modest, and strangely noble, like a peasant queen.

She terrified me.

Outside of *darshan*, I did my best to avoid meeting her on the stairs or in the garden. When I did, my legs shook and I couldn't talk. To make matters even more confusing, Mother Meera did not act like a guru. She did not spend her days on a dais surrounded by flowers, having her feet oiled. As Alexander had said, she did not give discourses, nor did she dispense advice. She made no rules, created no dogma, belonged to no religion, allowed no ashram to form around her. When people wished to dedicate their lives to her, she told them to go home and keep the faith they were born into, returning every now and then when they needed her help. Alexander told me that rabbis and Catholic priests came to visit, also Buddhists, Hindus, Muslims, Sikhs, Atheists, were all welcome—and Mother Meera never asked for anything in return.

During the day, she was always working, mixing cement, hauling bricks, hammering shingles on the roof, sweeping the porch, watering flowers. Completely ordinary except for the silent force that seemed to surround her.

Darshan proceeded like clockwork. Every night at seven, as the church bells rang in the distance, a door opened at the top of the stairs and Mother Meera descended, eyes lowered. What had only days before seemed the oddest thing in the world now began to feel quite natural, yet at the same time otherworldly, sacred, unfolding seamlessly as a dance. Whatever this woman was doing, she was doing it effortlessly and with complete authority. It was, indeed, impossible to imagine someone *not* in some altered state of consciousness sitting there hour after hour, taking head after head into her hands without wavering.

One evening, I came forward and knelt in front of her. Her fingers grasped my head. My mind raced with thoughts. I felt absolutely nothing. I looked into her eyes, expecting some kind of recognition, but I saw no one there. It was as if something were coming through her, watching me through her—or not me, but something within or beyond me. As Mother Meera stared, I noticed again that her pupils were indistinguishable, her face fixed like a mask, the irises vibrating back and forth. Afterward in bed, I read the following question and answer in a book about her:

> Question: When we have done pranam, we look into your eyes in silence. What are you doing?

> Answer: I am looking into every corner of your being. I am looking at everything within you to see where I can help, where I can give healing and power. At the same time, I am giving light to every part of your being, I am opening every part of you to light. When you are open, you will feel and see this clearly.

I decided that Mother Meera was some kind of phenomenon, a lusus naturae, a freak of nature, like the Amazing Kreskin or those people with enlarged pineal glands who are able to move iron carvings through glass with the tips of their fingers. There was no doubt that she was extraordinary; what I did doubt was my ability to believe that she was truly in contact with God. Even at this early stage of my spiritual journey, I was noticing a disturbing reflex in my psyche: every time I felt a kind of wonder, something in me rose up to crush it. In a fit of frustration with my hardheadedness, Alexander told me

I had a mind like a meat chopper. He was right: a part of me was too sharp, too eager to dissect, but that severity was the result of a sincere desire to understand. If Mother Meera was real, if this whole mystical worldview was real, it would break through my defenses.

On the afternoon of our departure for India, Alexander requested a private *darshan* for Mother to bless us on our trip. She came downstairs in her work clothes, sat on the *darshan* chair and took our heads in her hands. After she'd stared for longer than usual into our eyes, Mother stood and said, "Have a safe journey."

Alexander left me alone in the room. There were two portraits hanging on either side of the chair where Mother Meera had been sitting: one of her as a teenager, an enormous red *tikka* dot in the middle of her forehead, her face gentle and indulgent; the other a painting of Mr. Reddy in a white Nehru hat. I stared into her photograph for a long time in the quiet dark room, then had the impulse to place my head again on the pillow where Mother's feet had rested. Making sure that no one was coming, I knelt quickly in front of her chair and rested my forehead on the white pillow. Immediately, my ears filled with the same electric buzzing sound that had surprised me a week before. I stayed there, listening and asking inwardly to be shown what it was, imagination or something real. "I need proof," I said aloud. "Please, if you have any power at all, help me change."

When I lifted my head from the cushion, it was burning.

NINE

NDIA SMELLED OF barbecued bones and flowers, a composite perfume that wafted across everything: over dusty open lots, dark exposed skin, cattle, children, and piles of shit; over cracking buildings and rickshaw wallahs with spider-thin legs, puffing on crude cigarettes; over plump women with bellies spilling out of spumoni-colored saris; over ravenous dogs and beautiful teenage boys in loincloths, washing one another's sinewy backs at open waterspouts; over figures huddled around bonfires; over wilting temple gardens and holy men on the sidewalks, their faces painted like mandrills to honor their gods—Hanuman, Ganesha, Shiva, Kali. It was an otherworldly haze, like an incense ground from jasmine and charred remains, that colored my senses and softened them, drawing me into a strange, seamless, boundless world, unlike the one I knew—where holy men stayed in churches, lepers stayed in hospitals, cows stayed on farms, cars stayed in their lanes, and corpses stayed in morgues. Here, everything oozed, converged, and spread like an uncontrollable stew with all levels of life—animal, human, sacred, obscene, stinking, sweet, alive, dead—running together.

After a day's sleep in a fleabag motel off Connaught Circus in New Delhi, we went to a *khadi* emporium and bought several suits of Indian clothes, knee-length shirts, and matching baggy trousers.

"I don't know," I said to Alexander as I studied myself in the mirror, thinking that I wouldn't be caught dead wearing this in New York.

"It suits you," he said. "The *new* you. Swami Markananda," he added, bowing at the waist, then holding his hands together under his chin and shaking his head. "Welcome to my country."

After dinner in a back-alley restaurant, we walked arm in arm in the gardens behind the Red Fort. We were trying so hard to act like lovers, though the strain of our repeated failures to find happiness in bed was wearing Alexander down and filling me with shame. Since that first night in the loft—a tense, embarrassing preview of the melodrama to come—we had both known what we were up against and how unlikely it was that we could set it right. Still, we tried and tried, covering our mutual upset with excuses and apologies, vowing to transform this obstacle into an opportunity—*transformation* being Alexander's favorite word—and conjure desire into our heady relationship.

Sex wasn't the only problem between us, however. Dazzled as I was by Alexander's brilliance, I'd become aware as well of a flip side to his personality. His mood swings were sudden and unpredictable; one minute he'd be eloquent, funny, astute—and the next, he was fierce and accusing. He blamed his instability on the difficulties of our relationship—casting me in his romantic grand opera as the Hard-hearted Macho Enemy of Love, an embodiment of the male force he claimed was ruining the world. I tried hard to believe that Alexander's tirades were indeed a part of his genius, but wasn't always successful.

Still, that first night in India, drunk on the scent of jasmine, we were optimistic. The full moon was enormous and straw colored, low in the sky, casting an eerie brilliance over the garden as we strolled. Suddenly, out of the darkness, flashed the blinded white of a leper's eye as he held his thin arm out for coins. When I gave him nothing, he blessed me.

"I know what you're thinking," said Alexander. "You're thinking, how can anyone believe in God when there's so much agony in the world?"

I was getting used to the way Alexander anticipated my thoughts. "It *is* a valid question," I said.

"It is," he replied. "But it stems from a misunderstanding."

"Which is?"

"That God is only good. What so much western spirituality fails to teach us is that darkness—even the worst darkness—plays a crucial role in the creation. In the East, it's understood that God is light and dark, the nightmare *and* the dream. Horror has its purpose. So does evil."

"I'm not quite sure what that would be."

"The alchemists used to put a pinch of the blackest substance, what they called *nigra*, into their formulas for making gold. The Buddha wears a demon's mask on either side of his peaceful one. The goddess Kali has shark's teeth, and Christ surrounded himself with murderers and thieves. This is the secret of tantra, that shadow and light are sacredly linked. Are you with me?"

"Yes and no. The skeptic in me suspects that this is just a trick of the mind to justify evil."

"But genuine spirituality explodes ideas of good and evil," Alexander said. "Mother takes every head into her hands, however full of violence or fear, and embraces it. India has never viewed suffering as proof against the existence of God. On the contrary. She tolerates."

"Too much maybe. Look at the way these people live."

"But spirituality is about *fact*, not ideals. I'm saying that for all of her faults, this country has maintained a vision of the whole."

As we walked through the gardens, the Red Fort stood enormous and illuminated against the September sky. Old men on blankets offered us massages for ten rupees; couples nuzzled one another in the shadows. I understood Alexander's argument intellectually, but something in me balked at the insistence that pain, grief, and darkness were necessary aspects of human life. I had hoped that the path to enlightenment would end pain, not celebrate it, and articulated as much to Alexander.

"Let me tell you a story," he said, leading me to a place on the grass. "When I first went to Benares, I had two of the most frightening experiences of my life on the same morning. The first one happened at a place known as the Rat Temple."

"The Rat Temple?"

"Yes. Now I've always had a terror of rats, but I steeled myself to go there anyway. At first when I entered I could see nothing, and stood there on a platform looking into the darkness. Gradually, I began to see that the darkness was actually crawling with hundreds of thousands of rats that were fed and worshipped there."

Alexander paused for the full effect of this disgusting image to sink in.

"I felt challenged in a way I had never experienced before, and I learned a very important lesson. I realized that until I could bless even this horror, I knew *nothing*. Until I could look at the part of my psyche that *was*, figuratively speaking, an abomination of rats, I would never be truly awake. For that was the part of the human psyche that had created concentration camps, the part that was capable of any atrocity. Until I could bless even this, I could not transform it."

I hung on Alexander's words, revolted but fascinated, too, by the extreme truth of what he was saying.

He continued. "Once I was on a train with a man who had been among the first to go into Dachau after the war. He told me what it was like to come to the gates of this seemingly deserted place and then to see the people—what was left of them—stumbling out of those huts. All he could do was fall on his knees, as if he were praying, begging with every cell of his body for light and for healing. He said that it was the first time he had ever felt the existence of God."

"I'm sorry," I said. "But I don't really see how you got from genocide to God."

"Because *everything* is holy. Unless you go beyond your belief that a world with God would be a world without suffering, a big Disneyland where everyone gets in for free, you'll never understand that suffering is here to be used as fuel to awaken. Good and bad are human concepts. The Andromeda nebula is neither good nor bad. God is neither good nor bad. These words create false divisions. Of course, we must do what we can to relieve suffering every chance we get, but at the same time we need to accept that it will always exist, and *must*."

"But why?"

"Because it pushes us to grow. It pushes us to look for what exists beyond suffering. It pushes us to transcend our pain, and realize that we are more than the ego."

Alexander stopped speaking for a moment, then took my hand and turned me toward the moon, which was even lower now, hanging between the minarets of the Red Fort. "Do you see that light?" he asked.

"It's beautiful," I answered.

"Now, try to stop thinking for a second and just look at the moon. Try to empty your mind." I gazed up at the luminous circle.

"All right?" he asked.

"Yes," I replied, trying not to think.

"All right, then, now do your best to absorb what I am about to say without analyzing it."

"I'll try."

"There is no difference whatsoever between the light, the rat, you, and what the world calls God," Alexander said carefully. "The entire spectrum is contained within you, but your rational mind cannot contain this information. As long as your mind prevents you from seeing that you *are* a manifestation of that light—the intelligent, dynamic force creating *all* of this at every moment—you will *never* believe in God, nor should you."

Alexander paused and looked at me carefully, to make sure I was following.

"Go on," I said.

"All right. Let's try an experiment. I want you to go into the direct experience of this moment and ask yourself, 'Who am I?'"

"That's all I've been doing for twenty-eight years."

"No, it isn't, darling. You've never gone beyond the first step. Now, who are you?"

"I'm Mark Matousek."

"That's your name. Who are you?"

"I'm a man."

"That's your gender. Who are you?"

"I'm a human being."

"That's your species. Who are you?"

"I'm an inhabitant of planet Earth."

"That's your location. Who are you?"

I couldn't think of a response. "I guess I don't know," I answered.

"Exactly," said Alexander. "That is because you have never gone beyond the material part of yourself, the creature, the body. You don't understand that you are more than this form, with its senses, thoughts, emotions. You spin and spin in your little cage without looking outside it, or more deeply within. But, if you *did*," said Alexander excitedly, "you would discover something that would change your life forever."

"What?" I said. "Tell me."

"You would discover your real face in the mirror, a face more extraordinary than you can possibly imagine. It would be glowing with the awareness that you are *not* this limited thing. You're not even what people call the spirit."

"What the hell *am* I then?"

"That," said Alexander, pointing at the moon. "*Tat tvam asi*. That thou art."

I gazed up at the huge yellow orb, trying to comprehend what Alexander was saying. "That sounds like science fiction," I said.

Alexander laughed. "That's what skeptics have been saying about mystics since the beginning of time. The truth is so bright that it blinds the eye of reason. The ego-centered mind can't fathom the immensity. But I promise you, you are *not* this ego or this mind. You are *not* this unhappy collection of doubts, fears, hungers, and confusion. You are at the core of your being, that light. To realize that beyond your ignorance, you are, in fact, the very God in whom you so firmly disbelieve is to end one life and begin another. And that," said Alexander, turning me away from the moon and leading me down the path toward the door of the garden, "is the meaning of enlightenment."

*

Later, lying in the bed of our motel room, listening to the traffic noise of Connaught Circus, I thought about what Alexander had said. Was I really *that*? I wondered, thinking about the light of the moon, the force illuminating the very cosmos. Was that force the same as God, and was there really a way to connect to that bright source and live in a different way, beyond the confines of my mind? How wonderful if that were true.

Turning on my pillow toward the moonlight coming in through the motel window, I thought of the look in Mother Meera's eyes, the glimpse of brightness that I had seen there. I thought of her silence, the peace it brought. That feeling of peace was something that I could not doubt and that I could feel in my body even now. I thought of the words Alexander had spoken—*tat tvam asi*, that thou art—and repeating them again and again, I finally drifted off to sleep.

TEN

OUR PLAN WAS to ascend the Himalayas by bus from Kashmir, then to spend two months in Ladakh. Ladakh is a remote, rugged region, deep in the Himalayas, bordering on Tibet, that was an independent kingdom until the beginning of the nineteenth century. In 1833, it was annexed as part of the state of Jammu and Kashmir, which now belongs to India. For military and political reasons, the region was long isolated from the outside world, and its culture little known in the West.

Alexander couldn't wait to get me there. It was in Ladakh, shortly after the borders opened in the early '70s, that he had met his first teacher, a Tibetan Buddhist, and had begun his own spiritual education. Ladakh, as he described it, was a vast wilderness of desiccated landscapes, freezing winds, and monasteries frozen into the side of ancient mountains. It seemed cold, hard, alien, and the prospect of spending two months nestled among glaciers with no one to talk to except Alexander terrified me.

Nor was I comforted when he told me that Ladakh was the ideal place for exploding the ego.

"I don't want my ego exploding," I told him on the plane to Srinagar. "I want to be compos mentis."

"The ego and the mind are not the same thing," he answered.

"One is a torturer, the other is a tool. The torturer has to fry. That's what happens in Ladakh."

From Dal Lake, we boarded a third-class bus for our two-day, four-hundred-kilometer climb up the Zo-Jila Pass. Tucked between a stinking man in a dusty burnoose and a soldier in skin-tight army fatigues who spent the next fifteen hours scratching his prominent erection, we inched our way up the narrow mountain road, less than a foot from the edge of a railless drop of several thousand feet. As the temperature fell, the animals strapped to the roof began to scream, and the radio blared from oversized speakers above my head—Indian pop music reminiscent of the shrieks of little girls whose throats are being slashed. Alexander fingered his sandalwood-scented rosary beads and scribbled in his diary. I focused on the soldier to distract myself and tried to hold down the vomit that kept rising in my throat.

Leh, the capital of Ladakh, felt like an outpost on the moon: a rickety, filthy mess set against a vast lunar landscape of rocky desert, monolithic peaks and great sweeps of earth and sky. We dragged our suitcases along the main street of the town, past fetid sewers, ramshackle buildings, dusty streets, open bazaars filled with rancid cooking smells. Sinister-looking Kashmiri soldiers with rifles were posted everywhere, while Tibetan women with waist-length braids tied together against their backs stared at us, turning rosaries in their hands and muttering under their breath.

"What are they saying?" I asked Alexander as we passed a boarded-up video store and a group of teenage boys killing chickens by the stream.

"*Om mani padme hum*," he said, stopping to catch his breath. The oxygen level had dropped precipitously. "See that?" He pointed to a boulder carved from top to bottom with glyphs. I stopped and ran my finger along the letters. "It's the mantra of Padmasambhava," he explained, "the saint who brought Buddhism from India to Tibet."

"What does it mean?"

"There are many translations. What it comes down to is, 'I honor the Buddha nature within all things and the secret of the dharma that lies at the root of the lotus.' Something like that."

"All that in four words?"

"Four words, yes, but hidden in those words," said Alexander, putting his arm around my shoulder, "lies the mystery at the heart of the world."

We continued for half a mile out of town, until we came to the Dehlex Hotel: a dilapidated farm-pension with a vegetable garden and a spectacular panorama of the Karakoram mountain range rising twenty-five thousand feet in the distance. "Welcome to my second home," said Alexander, leading me to my room, an eight-by-four cubicle, sided floor to ceiling with glass. "Many things will change for you here."

He went upstairs to the second room we'd rented overhead. I sat on the cot and looked out at the mountains. *Om mani padme hum:* the words slid across my mind, hovered, rested, disappeared. Outside my window, an ancient woman stooped in the garden, pulling something from the ground. Her maroon clothing was washed out and dusty; she wore pointed shoes and beads on both wrists. Her fingers turned the beads as her lips moved, pulling at the roots. Her mouth never stopped. *Om mani padme hum.* A tiny donkey, no more than two feet tall, stood next to her, reaching up to chew on her braids until she swatted it and it bucked away among the purple blossoms and sunflowers. It was a vision of perfect harmony: the beads, her hands, her lips, the donkey, the flowers, the mountains, all bound together—I imagined as I lay there, exhausted—by those four words.

Maybe, I hoped, watching this peaceful scene, our time here would be wonderful.

The days were nearly identical. We rose early, bundled ourselves in layers of clothing, and left the hotel without washing. As October crept in, the weather grew colder and we didn't bother to undress at all at night, adding more layers day by day—like papier mâché—and waddling into town for tasteless pancakes and watery coffee at the Dreamland Restaurant. Then we separated, Alexander to his room, me to mine, for six hours of reading and writing.

Despite the harsh conditions and sporadic tensions with Alexander, those hours were manna from heaven for me. The day before leaving New York, I'd gone to a bookstore and bought everything that caught my eye: books on consciousness as well as classics I'd always wanted to read but never had time for. I'd carried those books halfway around the world to this glass room. Now I dove into Rilke's sonnets, Shakespeare's later plays, Eliade's works on magic, Evelyn Underhill's study of mysticism, Joseph Campbell's study of heroes, Freud's essay on the uncanny, and Jung's book on synchronicity. I read Elisabeth Kübler-Ross, Ernest Becker, Stephen Levine, and the *Tibetan Book of the Dead* to flesh out my understanding of the sacred relationship between mortality and enlightenment. I read *The Adventure of Consciousness*, a study of the work of Aurobindo Ghose, a modern-day sage and Western scholarly genius. I read several accounts of Westerners confronting Eastern wisdom—Isherwood's life of Ramakrishna, Lama Govinda's *Way of the White Clouds*, Osborne's life of Ramana Maharshi—and the works of Western mystics, such as *The Cloud of Unknowing* and Merton's *Seven Storey Mountain*, as well as works by saints themselves, the life of Anandamayi Ma and the dialogues of Nisargadatta Maharaj.

I read until I could hardly focus my eyes. I struggled to understand the language, the vision, that other *thing* to which Mother Meera had opened my eyes. I began to understand the validity and universality of my own longing, my darkness, my depression, and the accuracy of the intuition that had sent me out of New York: that, without this search, the things of the world, no matter how absorbing, were empty shells, dry as dust.

"There are rabid dogs in Gotsang," said Alexander on the bus. We were crossing the valley below in one of Ladakh's rickety transports, clinging to straps as dust blew through the cracked windows. "They travel in packs."

The bus dropped us off at the foot of a mountain where the trees were in full autumn glory, and we set off up the path with sticks, watching for red eyes, foaming mouths. The morning was crisp, sunny, the mountain's face striated in great sweeps of multicolored rock. The path continued up and up, through wind and gold and russet leaves. After almost two hours, we turned a corner and Alexander whispered, "There it is!"

First I saw nothing but rock and trees; then, just at the top of the promontory, the monastery came into view. It was extraordinarily lovely, set on a ridge just below the mountain's peak. As we approached, I saw that there were two buildings, the main hall and another small structure set off by itself. Reaching the top, we were welcomed by three monks who stood outside in their robes, bowing and making the *namaste* welcome sign. They must have been watching us climb for a long time.

"Far," I said, catching my breath. The monks smiled and cocked their heads, showing rust-colored teeth. "Very far up," I said, making the sign of a mountain with my hand.

"Yah, yah." They nodded. "*Chi! Chi!*" they said, offering us tea.

They led us into the dark interior of their sitting room, lit only by the slender openings of tiny windows and slats in the roof. We sat on the dusty floor close to the stove while the young monk poured us glasses of tea. I took a sip and nearly spat the warm, entrail-smelling stuff across the room.

"It's yak tea," Alexander whispered. "Try to look happy."

We left the room and walked over to the small building. There was a sentry at the door. "May I go in?" Alexander asked. The man looked him up and down with disapproval. "Please?"

He stepped aside and we ducked to enter the room, which was actually more of a cave, no more than seven feet in any direction. It was cold and extremely dark, a dirt floor, a row of butter candles on an altar with several ceremonial objects. I closed my eyes and instantly noticed a strange buzzing in my ears, an electrical humming like white noise, similar to the one I'd heard on entering Mother Meera's house. It had an automatic soothing effect on my mind, and I sat there for a long time, riding the sound in peaceful meditation.

When I opened my eyes, Alexander was prostrate in the dust, face down, arms outstretched. I looked at the sentry who was smiling at the sight of an Englishman lying flat out on the ground in his blazer and black shoes. When Alexander finally got up, there were tears in his eyes.

"Extraordinary," he whispered.

Afterward, on our way down the mountain, Alexander told me that a monk named Gotsang had sat in that cave for twelve years until his enlightenment. Since then it had become famous for its charged atmosphere. "The place where a person attains enlightenment retains that power of enlightenment," Alexander explained. "It's like a bomb explosion: the atmosphere is altered for hundreds of years. What most people don't understand is that enlightenment is a quantifiable, energetic phenomenon. It alters not only the person who awakens, but also his surroundings and the people who come into contact with him. That is how the light spreads."

I understood what Alexander meant. I had come to realize that seeing the brain as the center of consciousness was as misguided as believing that batteries create electricity. Consciousness was not *inside* anything; everything was inside consciousness. Our minds were moving in a greater Mind. It made perfect sense that when one conduit was cleared, the charge of the whole would increase. It made sense that when a man was liberated—when his mind had been cleared of obstruction—the vibratory state of the ground he sat on would be raised as well.

One day in the bazaar I bought a used pamphlet for one rupee entitled "Who Am I?" In eleven badly printed pages of dialogue with the modern saint Ramana Maharshi, I found the human condition summed up more concisely than I had ever seen it done before.

> *"Who am I?" asked the student.*
>
> *The master replied: "The gross body . . . I am not; the five cognitive sense organs . . . I am not; the organs of speech, locomotion, grasping, excretion, and procreation . . . I am not; the five vital airs . . . I am not; even the mind that thinks, I am not. . . ."*
>
> *"If I am none of these, then who am I?" the student asked.*
>
> *The master replied: "After negating all of the above-mentioned as not this, not that, the Awareness that alone remains— that I am."*

This passage echoed what Alexander had told me in the garden behind the Red Fort and appeared to be the simplest, most direct path to awakening that I had yet encountered. The primary tool of this practice was the question "Who am I?" which the student was encouraged to use as a scalpel to investigate himself, cutting through the illusory layers of his self-image in order to reveal what he actually is: pure consciousness, already enlightened. The seeker was instructed to use his most astute powers of observation and discrimination, *not* to have faith, *not* to believe, but to test, question, and deduce from his own scientific self-inquiry. The no-nonsense clarity of this practice inspired me and reminded me of the hours I'd spent as a child, gazing into the bathroom mirror, asking the very same question.

When I reported this to Alexander, he listened and smiled. "You have the makings of a *jnani*," he told me, explaining that, of the various paths of yoga developed to suit different spiritual temperaments, the path of discrimination suited me best. "*Jnanis* use their intellect to touch the source."

"It seems so easy," I said.

Alexander threw his head back and laughed. "That's what you think," he said.

Along with the awareness of another dimension, however, arose a painfully fractured view of *this* one and, in particular, my place in it. Removed from my familiar context, thrown into this existential quandary, everything was shifting so quickly inside me—not only my personal identity, but my fundamental understanding of what "reality" was in general. With each philosophical discovery I was making, the questions of where I fit into this expanding universe, and how I was going to live my life, became more complex. I understood my m.o. in the everyday world well enough, how to succeed in a system based on achievement, power, beauty, and so on. But the spiritual path turned all of that upside down, revealing that my former survival strengths (speed, cleverness, aggression) were actually handicaps. The mind I'd always prized for its sharpness seemed ill equipped for the kind of subtle, quiet apprehension that spiritual life called for.

What's more, the thought of a strictly religious life repelled me. I froze inside to think of the lives those monks at Gotsang led in their mountain aerie. A wave of pity, awe, and extreme sadness came over me at the thought that their long, lonely path might be the only way to God. I knew I could never live that way, never survive an endurance test of that kind.

It was also difficult not to compare myself to Alexander. He was Indian, I was American. He was a poet, I was a rationalist. He was an artist, I was an artisan. For him, the supernatural was natural. For me, it required deliberate and continual effort not to destroy every transcendental glimpse with doubt. If Alexander was a peacock, I was a dodo.

Though I was inspired by what I was learning, I was alienated by the lunar weirdness of Ladakh, which was mirrored in my relationship with Alexander. In the five weeks since we'd arrived, the breach between us had been steadily widening, intensified by our extreme isolation in this otherworldly place, the two of us locked in our separate quarters. The tension stemmed from sex, as always. The harder we tried, the worse it got, till we began to do everything we could to avoid one another. When Alexander did emerge from his room, he was wrapped in a black shawl like a woman in mourning; otherwise he was sprawled on the floor upstairs, obsessively throwing the coins of the *I Ching*, questioning the book's oracle for clues as to how we might wade through the swamp of emotions between us. Again and again, he threw the same hexagram: number fifty, the Cauldron. The image of burning up together in a pot was apt: being trapped at the top of the world with someone of Alexander's laser intensity did feel like being boiled alive.

One morning as we ate breakfast at the Dreamland, Alexander, looking particularly miserable, said, "I think we're each other's hired assassin."

"I thought we were trying to learn how to love each other," I said.

"It's not exactly working, is it?" Alexander looked away from me, out the restaurant window.

After breakfast, we walked back to the Dehlex in silence, past the skinny leper begging from his blanket, past the boys wringing chickens' necks by the river, past the ancient grandmother picking the seeds from dried sunflowers and reciting her mantra. At the door to my room, Alexander said, "I understand what's happening now," then turned to climb the stairs.

In the midst of this disorientation, my body seemed to be falling apart.

I needed meat. For a person raised on corned beef, kishka, and hot dogs, the sudden switch to the Ladakhi diet was catastrophic. After sampling the local mutton and spending three days clutching my stomach in bed, I'd been forced to limit my food intake to noodles, ghee, peanuts, and the occasional bowl of curd. I was literally, slowly, *starving*, and the hours when I wasn't in my room reading were spent frantically foraging through the restaurants and stores of Leh for something, anything, to satisfy my craving for familiar tastes. One afternoon in a curio shop, I found a can of tuna fish that had slipped behind a pile of newspapers. I tore it open with my Swiss Army knife and ate the greasy stuff with my fingers while the man behind the counter covered his mouth.

Oddly, the more I suffered the loss of creature comforts, the more oblivious Alexander seemed to become to his own physical body. He didn't seem to notice that we hadn't showered or changed our clothes for two weeks (ice-cold showers in the dirty stone stall down the hall, with the stench of the adjoining squat toilet, were out of the question). I hadn't seen my own legs since October. One day, when I did undress to relieve the itching, I was shocked at the sight of myself in the mirror. My abdomen had shrunk by half.

I ran upstairs to show Alexander. He was sitting on the floor surrounded by candles, incense, books, and torn sheets of paper, throwing the coins of the *I Ching*, his hair sticking out like a war bonnet.

"Look!" I said, pulling my shirt up over my belly.

He glanced up from his hexagrams and his mouth fell open. "I think you'd better see a doctor, darling."

"In Ladakh? I don't think so," I said. "Get me the hell out of this place!"

ELEVEN

THE NEXT MORNING, we boarded a plane for Madras, then hired a taxi to Mahabalipuram, where we planned to spend the next month. This was the idyllic India. I'd always imagined, rice paddies bordered by palms; shirtless, dark-skinned boys in ankle-length *lungis* walking by the side of the road, gauzy fabric clinging to their buttocks; women with baskets of bright-colored fruit; and the sweet warmth of the tropical air. As we sped along the highway, I breathed a sigh of relief to have escaped the eerie, other-worldly prison of Ladakh in one piece.

The town of Mahabalipuram, or Seven Pagodas, is halfway down the Coromandel Coast on the Bay of Bengal. Once the heart of the seventh-century Pallava Dynasty, Mahabalipuram is a smallish sea-side village famous for its temples and granite sculptures. In a taxi, Alexander told me that busloads of pilgrims arrived daily from all over India to visit these sacred spots, in particular the Shiva Temple, a thirty-foot pagoda-shaped structure located on the outermost spit of land at the edge of town. These pilgrims came to lay garlands around the necks of the stone bulls posted around the temple's perimeter and to pay their respects to the lingam hidden around back, a bul-bous black uprising of stone meant to represent the phallus of Shiva.

Indeed this phallic energy seemed to fill the air of Mahabalipuram itself; the beach seemed to breathe a hot, abandoned energy, like musk seeping into our pores. As soon as Alexander and I had settled into our waterfront motel, we threw off our clothes and ran into the water, jumping and screaming like children let out for recess. "I am Parvati," Alexander yelled, referring to Shiva's big-breasted consort. "My nipples birth a billion stars! The milk of my body feeds the cosmos!" Then he held his nose and slid backward underwater, pointing a toe like Esther Williams.

In Mahabalipuram, we were happier together than we'd ever been before, drunk on the beauty of the place. For the first time, our sex life began to improve, becoming almost effortless. Perhaps it was seeing Alexander here in the south, where he'd spent his childhood and was truly relaxed for the first time since I'd known him. Whatever it was, I felt genuinely attracted to him, and the satisfaction this gave us both was a welcome gift, a blessed respite after the storms.

"I kept hoping this beach would heal us," Alexander said to me one day as we were sunbathing.

"Me, too," I said, pulling him close. "Maybe we're not each other's assassin after all." I pushed the dark curls from the side of his face, admiring the cameo beauty of his profile. "Maybe we're actually sheep in wolf's clothing."

"Hmmmm," he sighed. "I like the wolf part."

In the course of those long, sultry days, I quickly recovered my weight and well-being. Every morning at eight, our boy servant brought us scrambled eggs and waffles and coffee. At midday, he reappeared with an enormous freshly caught broiled fish, french fries, ketchup, and Coca-Cola. In the evenings, we went to a café, where we ate from palm fronds, sliding rice and tandoori and chutney and curd around with our fingers, scooping the mixture into our mouths, then washing it down with quart-sized bottles of Kingfisher beer. It was in Mahabalipuram that I began to fall truly and passionately in love with Mother India.

This happiness was more than food, more than a tourist contentment, more than romance. It was a deep, welcome breath for my spirit. I decided to give up the quest for a time, to leave thoughts of enlightenment and mysticism behind, to stop reading and just let myself be. In this natural, relaxed environment, I felt my mind becoming tranquil, and the doubts and questions that had haunted me for so long began to melt away of their own accord.

There was an important lesson in this. "Happiness is the foundation of spiritual life," Mother Meera had said in her biography. *Happiness*, not striving, grasping, searching, suffering after an ideal. It bothered me that so much of the language of so many spiritual teachings was violent, referring to the annihilation of the ego, the dismemberment of vices, the death of the worldly self. It offended me, too, that these various prerequisites to awakening were said to be attained through the renunciation of the senses, which made the path to God seem barren, self-punishing, and no damn fun. The thought of spending the rest of my life opposing my natural impulses made my heart sink, while a path of joy inspired me and lifted my spirits.

Alexander had taught me much about this already, insisting as he did that piety had little to do with illumination, that life was a feast to be tasted and enjoyed with gusto and gratitude. Though we were not meant to be slaves to the senses, our bodies were intended to give us pleasure, not to be ridden, whipped, and discarded as nasty beasts. The physical world was a miracle after all—the material was as holy as the transcendent, *not* opposed to it. We had been given senses for a reason: to participate in this sublime creation, to see it for what it is—completely impermanent, but worthy too of celebration.

*

Ironically, no sooner had I relaxed my spiritual ambition, than I was caught off guard by the most extreme experience I'd had since beginning my journey.

Every afternoon just before dusk, after the pilgrims had left and the fishermen had parked their boats in the sand, Alexander and I would set out along the beach for an evening visit to the Shiva Temple. The beach was shaped like a scimitar, curving south toward Sri Lanka, with the temple set at its easternmost point. As we left our hotel one evening, we were struck by the unusual quality of the twilight, the opalescent sky descending into amber at the horizon, the temple silhouetted at the far end of the beach like a dark, erect nipple. The warm breeze moved gently through the palms to our right. On the left, hanging so low it almost touched the waterline, was the largest moon I'd ever seen, the color of yellow pearl. Alexander and I were so struck by the sight that we sat down at the water's edge to drink it in.

I stared for a long time at the moon, then closed my eyes. As soon as I did, Mother Meera's face appeared in my inner vision, converging with the moon's afterimage. Her face was alive, not photographic, and looking into her eyes, I felt my body leaning forward as if I were touching her feet at *darshan*. I laid my hands, palms down, against the damp sand, and in that second, a wave crashed, sending a shudder through the ground and into my body. Somehow that vibration through the earth, the sound of the wave, Mother Meera's face, and the light of the moon converged to jolt me awake.

When I opened my eyes, I was in an altered state. There was no hallucination, no vision, no distortion, just an intensification of sight, and a strange omniscience. My eyes were wide and unblinking; my field of vision was higher, deeper, and more lustrous, yet clearer

116

than it had ever been. The clouds, the moon, the water, my hands in my lap, all seemed to be pulsating together softly. I had the distinct impression of not simply seeing the surface of objects, but *knowing* them, apprehending automatically.

I stood and walked into the water up to my knees. "What is it?" Alexander shouted from behind me. There was an echo to his voice. "Tell me!" he said, but it seemed absurd to talk. I turned instead to the temple, walking unsteadily over the sand. I was perfectly aware that I was in a trance. Part of my mind was watching me weave my way along the beach. The sensation was not extreme—the sky did not peel back with fire; there were no bolts of thunder, no booming voices—but extremely subtle. I could feel things without using my hands, simply by looking softly enough. My breathing had changed, too: it wasn't me breathing, but me being breathed by the air around me, the palms, the waves. Everything was being breathed by that same breath that made the web by which these bodies were joined. I felt that if I moved my arm, it would somehow displace a branch in the tree next to me. The breeze itself seemed alive, intelligent.

This waking trance lasted for approximately twelve hours. In the course of the night, Alexander and I talked about what was happening, and happily, the sound of my voice did not dispel the state I was in. Neither did eating, drinking, washing, even sleeping. When I eventually drifted off, part of me stayed completely awake, watching me sleep. In the morning, when I woke up, there was a kind of afterglow, but the experience was over. I felt rested and completely unable to explain what had happened. But something *had* happened. Alexander had witnessed it. It was not my imagination. I had in no way engineered or anticipated this episode.

I realized, as I had in Mother Meera's house, but much more forcefully, that I was in a different ball game now, a different world where such shifts in consciousness were commonplace. I realized again that, in the face of this mystery, I knew almost nothing about what was really going on in this world, who I was, what life meant. What I did know was simply this: a process was taking place in me. I'd been taken up by something, but what it was and what to do with this information, I couldn't say.

Although Alexander and I wished that we could stay on in Mahabalipuram, he was running late on his story about the temples of Burma, which had paid for this trip in the first place. Unfortunately, no sooner had we left our magical beach than the spell between us was broken, and the conflicts that had plagued our relationship from the beginning began to erupt again. Removed from Shiva's playground in the south, and the hot, abandoned atmosphere that had melted our frigidity for a time, we were once again confronted with our sexual impasse, thrown into our respective pain and guilt.

Sex wasn't the only problem. Struggling and failing to couple with Alexander, I realized that although the details had indeed shifted from one lover to the next, the basic scenario was always the same with me. Challenged by Bob, Robert, various boyfriends and girlfriends, a part of me had always refused to surrender; there was a loner in me I could not share. Love affairs inevitably ended up feeling like three-legged races, and this feeling of entrapment inevitably forced me to break free. This pattern was in my wiring, it seemed, and Alexander was far too perceptive not to see it.

"I don't want to be wife number six," he used to joke, referring to King Henry. Alexander had indeed done everything in his power to keep the axe from falling, but even his forceful powers of persuasion couldn't stop me from leaving him.

We bottomed out at the Taj Mahal, where Alexander took me

on our last day in India, hoping for a romantic (temporary) farewell. The bickering started almost immediately, and after an hour of bitterly rehashing our relationship and coming to the same sad standoff, I turned to him and said, as gently as I could, "I think we should call it quits."

Alexander merely looked away from me at the lotus-studded pool that ran the length of the garden. "Of course you would."

"I'm so sorry."

"Are you now?" he spat back. "Are you really? I'm sure you always say that. Every time."

"Please, Alexander."

"Don't you dare patronize me."

I saw that there was no use trying to talk. For several minutes we stood there tensely next to the reflecting pool, then Alexander turned on his heels and walked quickly away from me, down the path toward the entrance of the Taj.

I stared up at the building's dome, like a great teardrop cast in white marble, regretting that I had spoken so abruptly. Would Alexander ever be able to forgive me? I wondered. What would I do without him in my life? I feared that without Alexander to cheer me on, the world would revert to its former flatness, the rainbow of possibilities I'd glimpsed the day we met in my office at *Interview* would fade again to earth tones. I watched his back as he strode away from me—and felt an awful sinking.

I followed him at a distance, and when he entered the room where Shah Jahan and his wife were entombed, I stood in the doorway, hoping he wouldn't chase me away. Alexander was circling the sarcophagus.

"He built all of this for her," he muttered.

I said nothing, fearing that he would explode.

He leaned against the far wall and faced me. "Imagine doing that for love," he said.

"You know that I love you," I said.

Alexander ignored this. "Did I tell you that the walls of this room were once covered from floor to ceiling with precious stones?"

"No."

"Imagine," said Alexander, gazing up at the vaulted ceiling, his eyes distracted. "Diamonds and rubies from Kenya, pearls from the waters off Sri Lanka, chryselephantine and teak from the forests of Madagascar—the rarest and most fantastic riches gathered from around the world to celebrate their magnificent union."

The walls were bare now. "Where did it all go?" I asked, looking around the empty room.

"Thieves stripped it away, of course." Alexander shot me a loaded look.

I said nothing. There was no way to confront him, I knew, without betraying the truth.

Finally, begrudgingly, Alexander turned to me and said, "I suppose we both got what we needed."

For my part, this was certainly true. But for him? "What did I give you?" I asked, half afraid of the answer.

He smiled sadly. "Another illusion to throw on the trash heap."

We hardly said another word for the rest of the day; finally, gradually, as the time for my departure the following morning approached, the tension between us seemed to ease a little. We ate in the same restaurant behind the Red Fort where Alexander had taken me our first night in India, and walked again afterward in the garden. But tonight there was no moon to light our way.

"Maybe," I said, when the silence became too heavy, "we can find some way to be friends." The cliché fell flat. "I really don't want to lose you."

Alexander shrugged.

"Dharma buddies or something," I said.

"Later maybe, after I forgive you," he said surprising me with a little smile. "I'm not a saint, you know."

"Oh really? And all this time I thought you were an enlightened master."

Alexander wagged his finger at me like a schoolmaster, the way he always did. "Of course, you'll have to be *severely* punished first, you know."

"I don't doubt it for a second."

"On your naked behind."

"I can hardly wait."

Then Alexander took my arm and led us toward the door of the garden.

The next morning, I left India.

PART THREE
SAVAGE GRACE

TWELVE

O N J U L Y 3, 1987, I flew back to New York after a rest period in Spain with no idea what would await me there. Sitting on the plane, studying my reflection in the window, I saw myself floating between two worlds—wondering which one I belonged in now. With no job, no apartment, no ambition, no money, I had no clue how I'd readjust to New York City, or how my old life would feel after this journey out—like the frog in Alexander's story, only I was falling back down the well after visiting the sea.

What's more, I wouldn't have Alexander there to cheer me on. Leaning into the cab window when we left each other in Delhi, he had taken both my hands in his and warned me that what awaited me in the West after this initial opening might be more difficult than I expected. "The world may seem alien for a while," he said as the driver smoked his *beedie* and watched us in the rearview mirror. "Everyday things may seem unreal for a while. You'll find yourself doubting everything. It's part of the process." Then Alexander kissed me gently on either cheek, handed the driver a hundred-rupee note, and said, "I'll be in touch."

Had I an inkling of just how prophetic Alexander's words would be, I might have turned back at JFK.

"You're a walk-in," James said when he saw me the next day.

"What do you mean, a walk-in?" I asked.

"A person whose body has been taken over by another life form," he said, studying me carefully. "You're completely different."

James was the only person I knew who I thought might understand how strange I was feeling. Before leaving New York, I'd given him addresses in India and Europe where I could be reached; letters with his delicate, familiar handwriting were waiting for me along the trail in Paris and Ladakh. These letters were full of encouragement and quotations, each marked at the end with James's trademark signature: a thumbprint in red ink circled with the word EVIDENCE. These letters established James as my only dharma brother back home, and now, as we sat in his studio apartment on Charles Street, it seemed odd that we were actually here, in the flesh, facing each other across his table.

Still, I might have attributed James's remark to his dramatic flair had I not been approached a few days later at the Russian Baths on East Tenth Street by Cho, a Korean dancer I'd met only twice before. When I ran into him coming out of the steam room, Cho walked straight over with an amused expression on his face. He pointed to the middle of my forehead, folded his hands across his bony chest, and smiled mischievously. "Where have you been?" he asked.

"To India."

"Ah." He nodded, as if that explained everything. "Very different," he said, pointing again at the spot between my eyebrows. "Bigger."

"Bigger?"

"Much light," he corrected himself. Cho scrutinized my forehead as if he were studying something he could actually see. "Big light!" he laughed.

Carole didn't see it; she was too busy shrieking when I surprised her at her door with a poster of Ganesha held over my face like some-one in a Hindu production of *A Chorus Line.*

"Oh, my God!" she screamed, throwing herself at me, hugging me so hard I couldn't breathe. "I don't believe it!"

"Ouch!"

"I didn't think you were ever coming back."

"Didn't you get my letters?"

Carole pointed to the stack of envelopes stuffed in an enamel cow on her counter. "You sounded like you were in hell in Ladakh."

When tensions reached their peak with Alexander, Carole was the one I wrote to; long whinning letters like a newlywed son to his mother after marrying the wrong girl. "It wasn't right," I said.

"Of course it wasn't; anybody could see that. You're both too intense. Did you hear about Andy?" I already knew that Warhol had died mysteriously that winter after a routine gall bladder surgery. "You think it was AIDS?" she asked.

I didn't. Andy had always claimed to be celibate—at least that was the buzz around the office. In one of his famous Zenlike asides, Andy had once said that sex was really just "the memory of sex"—whatever that meant—and though his platonic lover had succumbed to the virus the year I left *Interview,* it seemed unlikely to me that Andy had been infected. Now, thinking of my ex-boss, I remembered how obsessed he'd been with his own immortality, going so far as to arrange for time capsules containing his papers, mementos, and effects to be buried a hundred feet underground so that future gen-erations would not forget him. Now Andy was gone at fifty-seven, a strange, unexpected end to a very strange life.

"I wonder who else is gone," I said, noticing for the first time that Carole had acquired cheekbones in my absence. "You know, *you're* very thin."

"Ten pounds," she said, sounding surprised herself.

"A little too much, maybe?" Carole, who normally looked fifteen years younger than she was, was not looking her best. Besides the thinness in her face, the paleness of her normally ruddy complexion, her lips were cracked and dry. She seemed tired, somehow, and smaller than I remembered her.

"So?" I asked.

On the table next to the sofa was the photograph of Mother Meera, looking beautiful in a purple sari, that I had sent Carole from Germany. It was framed, with a candle and an incense holder beside it, like a miniature altar. Carole had gone to Thalheim for two weeks while I was in India, and I was dying to know what had happened.

She described her trip: getting lost on the train from the airport (a week hardly passed when Carole did not get lost somewhere), the one-armed man who "accidentally" found her wandering, jet-lagged, through the streets of Limburg and drove her to Frau Schneider's pension, where her alarm clock didn't go off and she almost slept through *darshan*. Carole described running across the fields from Dorndorf to Thalheim in the pouring rain and finding Mother Meera's house, stepping into the foyer—where her ears instantly started ringing, just as mine had—climbing the stairs through the eerie quiet, peeking over the banister and catching sight of Mother Meera for the first time. Whereas I had seen in this tiny figure a majestic presence, Carole had seen something completely different; she saw Mother Meera as a child, and this image touched her deeply.

"I couldn't stop crying," Carole told me. "It was awful. People were staring. When I saw her, it was like someone stuck a needle through my chest."

"I know."

"She looked so tiny in her sari. I remembered the orphans I used to work with in the foundling hospital, the way they'd sit there in their cribs hugging themselves and rocking, like someone was holding them. I realized that a part of me was just like those little babies, rocking myself, feeling so lonely."

Carole blew her nose. "It was ridiculous. I didn't think I'd be able to go up in front of all those people sobbing like that. Plus I was scared of her. I thought she was going to melt me."

"What do you mean, melt you?"

"In a puddle. Like the witch in *The Wizard of Oz*. She was going to take one look at me and—" Carole did her imitation of Margaret Hamilton dissolving, waving her arms, screaming for help. "They'd have to take me out of there in a bucket."

"You're crazy."

"Did you see the way her pupils quiver back and forth when she looks at you?" Carole asked. "It's like she's really seeing something."

"Your soul."

"Maybe. Do you believe it?"

"I have no idea what I believe."

Carole picked up Mother Meera's picture and studied it. "So much love," she said.

"Maybe. But it's not really personal. She just seems to love in general, like the queen of England. She doesn't know who she's waving to from the car; she just waves; she's the queen. That's what Mother Meera's like, I'll bet. She doesn't really know who we are."

"Or maybe she knows *exactly* who we are," Carole suggested. "Maybe she does really see our souls."

"Now *that*," I said, "would be really scary."

My first order of business was to find a place to live, and since I had almost no money and no prospects for earning any, I appealed to

Robert to let me sleep on his couch. Robert and I had lived together as lovers years before, when I first came to New York. We had parted amicably—our Wasp divorce, we called it—and never lost touch, falling into a brotherly friendship that suited us better than romance ever had.

Some things, however, had not changed—including Robert's practicality about money. Not long after I'd settled into his place, hoping that I could coast for a while until I had some clue as to what to do next, Robert sat me down and made it clear that as much as he would like to support me in my quest for higher consciousness, he couldn't. He suggested that I approach editor friends for free-lance writing jobs. But going back to celebrity journalism was out of the question. I had no intention of slipping back to my old life; the thought of limousine chasing made me scream. Passing headlines like CHER GETS A TUMMY TUCK at the newsstand, I crossed myself and thought, I'd rather die. I was determined to find a new way to make money as a writer, to discover some means of writing about things I cared about—subjects with heart and conscience—in the monthlies of Babylon. But how?

I was thinking about this one day as I left Central Park and walked east to Madison, wandering aimlessly down through the fifties, staring up at Trump Tower—gold against a clear summer sky—thinking, "What am I doing here? Am I out of my mind? What *is* this?" The sidewalk was swarming with people, career women in Reeboks and Chanel suits, eyes darting, men with big bellies popping out of button-down shirts shoving hot dogs in their faces next to foul-smelling vendor carts, taxis honking and braking and screeching—the whole lunatic mess of this place I'd once loved so much but felt, in that moment, so estranged from.

I let the river of people carry me past Bijan and Chloe and Saks.

At the Condé Nast building, I stopped and gazed through the revolving doors, then crossed the street and looked up at the windows, thinking of all the people I knew in there, most of whom had been promoted, were getting married, buying houses in the Hamptons and condos on the Upper West Side, rising through the ranks of this building like planes waiting their turn on the runway. I wondered if they were happy at their desks, satisfied with their titles and Belgian slippers, walls plastered with glossy covers; if they were secure and content in this familiar world, happy to know what their future held. Or were they, as I had been, staring out their windows, feeling empty and tired and lost and sad, hungry for adventure, overdosed on hype and deadlines, wondering at what it all meant and how it was passing by so quickly?

Just then, I heard cymbals and chanting. I turned and saw a group of Hare Krishnas dancing up Madison Avenue in their orange costumes and shaved heads, barefoot, beating tambourines. The traffic on the sidewalk paused to stare and let them pass.

"Hare Krishna, Hare Krishna, Krishna Krishna, Hare Hare!" the group sang out, leaping in circles, laughing, happy. A girl who looked like Sinead O'Connor trailed behind, distributing flyers, which people mostly refused, or crumpled in their hands without reading. When she passed me, our eyes met—she smiled as if she recognized me, and I smiled back. "*Om, shanti,*" she said to me—peace, my friend.

"*Om, shanti,*" I answered back, taking the paper from her hand. The girl looked at me a few seconds more, then folded her hands in the traditional way and caught up with the rest of the group.

For a second, I wanted to run after them, shave my head, surrender to devotion. Their path, in that moment, seemed so simple— they'd made a choice to renounce the world; they knew where they belonged, what they believed in; they weren't on the fence, trying to have it both ways. A thought flashed through my mind: get out now before it's too late. But even as I thought it, I knew that this was not my path. I had to be amphibious, to find a way of breathing in both elements, move in and out of both worlds. I couldn't drop out: I had to drop in and smuggle what I knew in with me.

"Mark?" The sound of my name snapped me out of this reverie. I turned and saw my old friend Joe looking handsome in a tailored suit.

"Look at you," I said, shaking his hand, becoming suddenly self-conscious in my T-shirt and sweatpants. "Very impressive." The last time I'd seen Joe, he was my underling at *Interview*. Now he was the arts editor at *Harper's Bazaar*.

"Come write for me," said Joe.

"I can't."

"You're under contract? Who got you?"

"Nobody. I'm totally broke. But I just can't do that shit anymore." Joe winced when I said the word *shit*. "I don't mean that *you're* doing shit," I started to explain, but Joe held up his hand, knowing what I meant.

"Got it," he said. "What about books?"

"I'd like to write books."

"I mean, what about covering books for the magazine?"

I looked down at our feet next to one another on the sidewalk, one toe sticking out of my filthy sneakers, next to his Paul Smith boots. At a dollar a word, I couldn't say no.

Since my return, I'd been receiving letters from Alexander several times a week. They ranged in tone from passionate to ominous—full of psychological analysis and spiritual advice—and though I was grateful for Alexander's continuing interest in my spiritual education, I found his letters upsetting, too. One in particular had me worried. Scrawled in his nearly illegible hand on blue aerogram stationery—the outside of the envelope covered with afterthoughts and quotations—it read: "I threw the I-Ching three times for you today, and every time it came up with hexagram #36, DARKENING OF THE LIGHT. Be extremely careful, my friend. You may be moving into treacherous waters."

THIRTEEN

A MONTH AFTER my return to New York, the phone rang at a few minutes past midnight. It was Carole, sounding breathless.

"I couldn't get up the stairs just now," she wheezed into the receiver.

"What's wrong?" I asked, disoriented by the dream I'd been having when the phone woke me.

She didn't answer. Then, through the covered receiver, I heard her crying. "What *is* it?" I asked again.

"I think I'm really sick."

First thing the next morning, I went to Carole's apartment and found her flat on the couch, looking terrible. She was drenched in sweat and shaking, a heavy sweater around her shoulders. "I'm freezing," she told me, hugging herself. I covered her with an afghan and slipped a thermometer under her tongue. The mercury registered 104. I got her doctor on the phone.

"It's probably just the flu," he said. "Keep her warm. Plenty of fluids."

"Isn't this dangerous?" I asked, meaning the fever.

"It's good that it's spiking. That means it will break. Don't worry."

I passed this information on to Carole, who didn't believe it. "I know . . . what . . . the flu feels like," she said, so short of breath that she couldn't finish a sentence. "This is not the flu."

I sat with her for the rest of the day and through the night, assuring her that this bug was going around. I put a towel on the floor and sponged her with alcohol to bring the fever down, but this only cooled her off for an hour. When the fever was the same the next morning, I started getting worried myself.

"Maybe it's pneumonia," her doctor conceded when I called again. "Bring her in when she can walk."

The word raised the red flag. When Carole heard it, she covered her mouth with the blanket. "It couldn't be," I told her. "Not a chance."

"What about that guy?" asked Carole. Three years before, she'd had the only one-night stand of her life, with a gorgeous man she met at a disco, shortly after she was divorced. Both of them were too drunk to think about rubbers. "He could have given it to me."

"Impossible," I said. The chances of Carole having the virus were one in a million. To satisfy her, I called the AIDS Hotline, and spoke to a perky girl who told us—after hearing my description of a forty-two-year-old, heterosexual, non-drug-using woman with fewer than five sexual partners in her life—not to give it another thought.

This was impossible, of course—once the seed of the idea had been planted, neither of us would be satisfied until the possibility was ruled out. The next day, when the fever had barely dropped, I bundled Carole up and took her in a cab to the NYU hospital, where she was admitted for observation. Her doctor, who was visibly worried by how sick Carole looked, ran a battery of tests and told us to wait in the lounge until the results were in.

Carole was petrified. I was nervous, too, but did what I always do in situations where people are falling apart: got rock solid. I flipped on Oprah to pass the time, and we sat there watching as a transsexual

135

couple—the wife was a former man, the husband a former woman—
fielded questions from the audience about how they'd adjusted to living together in an Arizona suburb. The wife, who was six foot three
and looked like a beagle, told Oprah that she couldn't understand
why the community was having such a hard time accepting them.
"We're just like everybody else," she said, dabbing at her eyes as the
camera went for a closeup.

"Poor thing," said Carole.

Halfway into the five o'clock news, the phone rang. It was the
nurse, telling us to come downstairs immediately.

Carole sat on the examining table, her bare legs dangling over the
edge, a sweater around her hospital gown, clutching my hand as we
waited for the doctor. Finally, he entered, closed the door, and leaned
against it with a file folded across his chest. In a voice as flat and disin-
terested as someone ordering lunch at McDonald's, without looking
Carole in the eye, he said, "It's Pneumocystis, ma'am."

Carole looked confused. "What's that?"

"You have AIDS, ma'am."

Carole gasped. I stopped breathing. The doctor fixed his eyes on
a point somewhere beyond both of us.

The irony was too outrageous; I was stunned, and in the hours
and days after we got the news, I went over it a hundred times in my
head, trying to make sense of why it was Carole and not me on that
examination table, getting that diagnosis. I'd fucked my way around
the globe for fifteen years, sampled every kind of man or woman
who caught my eye, body fluids flying, while Carole was trapped in
a house in the suburbs, gritting her teeth through the weekly ordeal
of watching her impotent husband grind and yank himself into dry

semitumescence. Yet here I sat, healthy as a horse—outwardly, at least—while she was stricken.

"Thank God we never slept together," I thought. There had been one near miss two years before when Carole, loose on sangria, had begged me to make love to her. I refused, knowing what trouble it would lead to; I'd learned from past mistakes that when a gay man sleeps with a woman who's devoted to him, it's the woman who ends up paying the bill. Carole and I were walking a fine line between friendship and obsession as it was, and besides, I had told her then, I wouldn't take the chance of infecting her. Fortunately, I managed to steer through the tense moment with my pants up, and we never mentioned it again. Now I was grateful for that stubbornness. If Carole and I had been sexual that night, I would have always believed that I had destroyed her life.

Nonetheless, the turnaround of our present situation was unreal for both of us—extremely confusing, almost perverse. It was so strange, in fact, that we couldn't help but wonder whether some mystery wasn't at work between us. "I feel like this is why we met," she said, without explaining what she meant. I had a similar intuition.

In any case, Carole and I had more immediate things to do than speculate on fate: namely, how to break the news to Carole's grown daughters, Jamie and Marcy; how to proceed with treatment for the pneumonia; how to find a way through the depression that closed over Carole's head the day that she went home from the hospital. She was shattered, and though I was worried for the state of her body, I became even more alarmed, in the weeks after the diagnosis, by the state of her mind—the impression she had that she had lost her identity now that she knew a virus was inside her; that, becoming a person with AIDS, she had ceased to be herself. The world was suddenly split for her, she said, between those who were living and those who were leaving, and the woman she'd been a month before, with a life expectancy of forty more years—a "normal" woman with two grown daughters and a crucifix around her neck—had slipped away into that other zone, the have-not zone, the dying zone.

With death suddenly shoved in her face, Carole began to question her very existence, as I had done after that morning in Jamaica with John. She found herself sinking deeper and deeper into despair, feeling that she had no more reason to go on.

"The girls are grown up," she said to me after the pneumonia had cleared up. We were sitting in the stairwell outside Robert's apartment, her head on my shoulder. "They don't need me anymore."

"We all need you."

"You don't need anybody."

"You don't believe that."

"At least, you don't think you do."

This had been Carole's primary complaint about our friendship from the beginning: that I was aloof, here today, gone tomorrow. When I walked out the door, she said, I never looked back, and when we parted, she was always afraid that she might not ever see me again. She was right in a sense—part of me did resist attachment—but what Carole didn't realize was that this was changing very quickly. Since the day of her diagnosis, I'd begun to see her, and my connection to her, much more clearly. I'd begun to realize, for the first time, how much I actually loved her, how much I relied on her for roots, for comfort and a home. "That isn't true at all," I said.

"I just don't know who I am now," she said.

I looked at her sitting there with her chin resting on her knees like a teenager. She was in her favorite outfit—an old work shirt of mine, Girbaud jeans. She had on her diamond earrings, her emerald ring, mascara, the lipstick we'd picked out together at Barneys. Her gray roots needed to be touched up.

"Want to know something?" I said. Carole looked at me with red eyes. "You're the same person you were before."

The words were like magic; the minute I'd said them, I saw the change in Carole's expression. She sat up straight and lifted her chin. "You're right," she said. "I'm still me, goddammit."

The obvious thing for me to do was be tested for the virus myself, but I put it off, rationalizing that as long as I behaved as *if* (read: wore a rubber), there was no reason to stress myself out with the formality.

Nonetheless, I had lost a lot of weight in India and reported to the doctor who'd treated John before he died. Dr. Weissman took blood and urine samples, looked at me inside and out, told me everything looked perfectly normal.

"Eat more ice cream," he said, feeling under my armpits, lingering over something.

"What are you feeling?" I asked.

"Nothing," said Dr. Weissman.

"You can't feel nothing."

"A slight inflammation. Nothing to worry about."

I reached under my armpit and felt the lump he'd found. It was soft, about the size of a Reese's peanut butter cup. "You sure?" I asked.

"Just a swollen gland," he said.

When I was dressed and we were sitting in his conference room, I told Dr. Weissman about Carole. I told him that most of the time I was resigned to the fact that in all likelihood, I had HIV, but that sometimes, when I wasn't expecting it, I had a biological panic—an animal fear that seized and shook me at the sight of someone I'd known once in healthy times dragging down the street with a cane, eyes vacant, covered with sores. "When I'm not expecting it. Or in the middle of the night. Or I think of John at the end, panting like a dog."

Dr. Weissman listened attentively. He was a small, bald man with a moustache and (as John once reported enviously) a season box at the Met. I felt comfortable with him and told him everything that was on my mind. When I was finished, he suggested gently that taking the test might not be a bad idea.

"I'll let you know when I'm ready," I said.

"In the meantime, I want you to remember something," Dr. Weissman cautioned, looking at me across the desk. "There are two diseases going on here. There's AIDS and there's the fear of AIDS. Both of them are epidemic. Keep them separate, if you can."

I tried to follow Dr. Weissman's advice, for myself *and* for Carole, who fell into a busy routine of visits to practitioners—acupuncturist, internist, nutritionist, masseur, psychotherapist—reporting to me at the end of the day on any new developments. In the meantime, I tried to circumnavigate the issue of being tested by devouring the words of enlightened masters, attempting (clumsily) to meditate and practice yoga, and generally sticking to my inner life so I didn't have to deal with more earthly matters—namely, sex.

I wasn't always successful.

One day, as I was crossing Sheridan Square, a preppy-looking blond boy in Weejuns and a twill shirt left his stool at the falafel place and made a beeline to the corner where I was waiting for the light.

"Excuse me, *sir*," the boy said, emphasizing the last word. "Do you know where the S&M store is?"

He said it matter-of-factly, staring straight at me with turquoise eyes, like someone playing a schoolboy in a J. Crew catalog.

My legs went numb and my pants caught fire.

"You mean the place with the leather masks in the window?" I answered as coolly as possible.

"Yeah," he said, his eyes passing slowly from my face, down my chest to my crotch. "That place."

"I think it's down there," I said, nodding my head toward the river, knowing full well that it was.

The boy stepped toward me, standing several inches from my face, and slowly, audaciously, reached out and unbuttoned the top two buttons of my shirt, which was closed to the collar. "Wanna show me?" he asked.

We turned and walked together down Christopher Street. I saw the boy watching me out of the corner of my eye. "I love it," he said.

"Love what?" I asked, suddenly so turned on I was dizzy.

"Getting tied up. Being a slave." I looked over at the kid, who gave me a naughty smile. "You can do whatever you want to me. Okay?"

"Okay," I said.

We had arrived at the Leather Man. There was a male mannequin hanging upside down in a harness in the window with something that looked like a colander strapped to its ass, and handcuffs around its wrists and ankles. Its head was covered with a black ski mask with holes cut out for the nose and mouth. The boy studied the window display. "Looks like fun," he said, leading me into the store.

Glass cases overflowed with sadomasochistic paraphernalia: leather clothing with studs and without, masks, whips, chaps with cutouts for butt and genitalia, send-ups of various macho costumes (cop, jock, and cowboy), dildos piled in vats, some of them thicker than my calf (black, white, veined, smooth, single-, double-, and triple-headed)—dildos with batteries, and dildos with balls; there were torture devices, weights to hang on the balls, things that looked like fishing tackle for rectal insertion and piercing, suction syringes to stretch the cock, suction cups to stretch the nipples, masks with nose holes and eye holes, belts with terrifying buckles, lotions that burn and lotions that numb, ersatz poppers—a pharmacopeia of dangerous fun.

The boy was mesmerized. He took something that looked like a Ping-Pong paddle off the wall and slapped his hand with it hard. "Whoa," he said, impressed by the pain or the sound or both. "We're gonna have a good time, Daddy."

I was getting very uncomfortable—hot and scared at the same time. As I followed the boy down the narrow spiral staircase into what I assumed would be a retail dungeon, Mother Meera's face flashed through my mind. What was I doing here? I wondered. What did all these weapons mean? Who was this kid who wanted to be my slave, and why did the thought of hurting him at his own request make me feel so sickeningly hot?

I felt myself being torn in half—one side wanted to throw myself into this pit, with a boy who wanted to get on his knees and beg, and not to care what it might mean. That side, which held me like a magnet to the boy as he ran his fingers over a fifteen-inch black dildo sticking out of the wall, wanted to be brutal, to fuck the kid (and the entire world until it screamed); to see myself reflected in his victim's eyes, huge and thick and totally *male*, to make myself *felt*, leave my mark, wipe myself off, and not look back. But intense as this dream of power was, there was another voice in me now, subtler but impossible to ignore. It repeated, *This is sad, empty, wrong.* It said, *This way lies disaster. Make your choice. Make it now.*

I took a last look at the kid's ass in his gym shorts, the faint golden baby hairs on the backs of his calves. He looked over his shoulder from the toys he was pretending to study on the wall and winked. "I'll just be a minute," I said to him, winking back. I turned and walked quickly out of the basement, then raced up the stairs two at a time, out of the store, down Christopher Street, and up the stairs of my apartment, bolting the door.

What was I really so afraid of? I wondered afterward. An hour of slapping and make-believe violence? Beating my chest and beating my meat? Not really. The panic I felt after this incident had much less to do with the actual situation than it did with the brutal feelings the boy aroused in me. It was almost as if I could make out a bestial image leering at me from around the corner of my psyche. I'd seen Mr. Hyde before, of course—lived with him, if not happily, at least indulgently, all my life. I'd given in to his whims for as long as I could remember, covering his excesses, abuses, betrayals as best I could; and when I couldn't, writing off these mistakes as par for the course for a horny guy playing by the law of the jungle.

But so much had changed. Deliberate unconsciousness of what I was doing and *why* was no longer possible. Obviously, I couldn't focus on waking up with one half of myself, and on oblivion with the other. Though I didn't have a clue how to reconcile the devil and the angel inside me, I knew I had to try.

As outwardly innocent as the meeting with the boy had been, it reminded me that there was a dark man standing in the doorway between me and myself, and until I did real battle with him, I would remain stranded.

Somehow Alexander picked up exactly what was going on. In his next letter, he wrote, "Getting clear is excruciating, like going through a fire. It has to be because evil is very powerful. When we finally stop masking *anything* from ourselves, then we can change. The key to the garden is terror at oneself."

FOURTEEN

DECIDED TO be celibate. Until I figured out how to proceed with sexual life as a person on a spiritual path, it seemed like the only possible course of action.

The failure of my relationship with Alexander had made me realize how bound together love, hate, and sexual anger were inside me, how invariably I grew to despise the people I loved, reflexively, the deeper they touched me. I felt powerless to stop this reaction, and it ruined most of my closest relationships. There was a strange barrier of intensity around my heart, as if it were surrounded by fire. Lovers had to pass through this blaze of resistance again and again before they got through. Unfortunately, by the time the ordeal was over, most of them were so burned, and I was so ashamed of my behavior, that we couldn't love each other anyway.

Sex invariably became an obstacle for me in exclusive relationships, desire seemed almost antithetical to love. Lust was always unmanageable, a fierce, anarchic hurricane of energy that swept me along like a drunk, leaving me in a haze, looking at what I'd done—or *whom* I'd done—almost as if the act had been carried out by someone else. Instead of feeling *more* when I was on the make, as I imagined "normal" people did, my feelings seemed to stop when my cock got hard. I went blank, robotic, a weird sort of euphoria driving my body toward its target like a predator.

I wasn't a sadist exactly, but as the boy on Christopher Street reminded me, I knew the potential was in me. I had let that monster out of the cage only once, at sixteen. An older guy and his teenage lover had picked me up for a three-way. While the cute kid and I sat in the living room smoking a joint, the older guy disappeared. Soon, I heard moaning sounds coming from the bedroom.

"What's that?" I asked.

"He wants us to beat him up," the kid said.

The moans got louder. "He loves it," he snitched. "What about you?"

"Okay," I said, not sure what to expect.

In the bedroom, the man was naked on his stomach, rolling his ass around with a pillow under his hips, making these ridiculous noises. I looked at him and then at the kid, who walked over and slapped him hard on the ass. The old guy went crazy, bouncing his flabby white butt up and down, holding his hands behind his back.

"Do it," he whispered to me.

Timidly, I stood next to the bed and slapped the old man's ass.

"Harder," he begged.

I did it again, a little harder. Then something seized me; I got absolutely furious at the man on the bed for wanting me to hit him, and this fury made me hit him really hard. "You stupid jerk," I said, punching his ass with my fist.

"I'm stupid. I'm stupid," he groaned.

"I'll give you what you want, you asshole," I said, pulling his head back by the hair. The more I talked, the more he moaned; the more I slapped him, the angrier I got, until I was out of control, on the bed, whipping the guy with my shoe. I don't know what happened exactly, but the next thing I remember, the kid was grabbing me, the old guy was curled up in a ball with his hands over his face, and I was being thrown out of the house in my underwear, my hands still clenched in fists.

"Fucking sicko," the kid said as he threw my clothes out the door after me. "Take a fucking hike."

I hoped that celibacy would clear my mind of its sexual mania and help me understand the breach that seemed to exist between my heart and my penis. Though I had no intention of becoming a renunciate for pious reasons, I knew that I had to find the joy in sex, the love in it. I hoped that by putting myself out to pasture, I'd be able to figure out why this joy had eluded me thus far.

My confusion boiled down to the age-old question of what, if anything, sex had to do with love. The answer seemed to be very little; given their choice, the majority of the men I knew would much rather get naked with a stranger than with a soul mate. But why? Was this testosterone taking the path of least resistance, the natural path for animals programmed to scatter their seed? Or were we also programmed for a loftier exchange of heart and soul; meant to use our bodies, in fact, like radios, to communicate a higher love? Weren't we meant to aspire in this direction, at any rate, to integrate the contradictory aspects of our being—infusing numen into flesh—and find the middle path where the two could walk in harmony?

I made a note in my journal: sex death, enlightenment. These issues, I saw, were the points on the triangle forming my life, the interlocking, progressive steps on my soul's journey. Sex had led me to the prospect of death, and death would lead me toward enlightenment if I took its lessons to heart and let them burn me into awakening. If I could only crack this puzzle and understand the relationship between sex, death, and enlightenment, I sensed that an enormous healing would take place, freeing me of a grief that had begun when

I was a boy, fracturing my vision of the world, making me feel like an orphan in the universe—always outside, always hungry—erasing me from the memory of God. My attitude toward sex was central to this cynicism, and it was here that a real transformation must begin.

I first heard Ariel Jordan's name from a friend of Robert's, who told me that this was a man I had to meet. Two years after my return to New York, she finally introduced us.

Jordan was an elegantly dressed, silver-haired Israeli in his early forties who had made award-winning documentary films in Israel before migrating to the states in the early eighties. When we met, he obviously knew something about me from our mutual friend.

"We need to talk," he said, after hugging me hello. He was handsome, commanding, and straight. "Maybe you'd like to see my work?"

"What kind of work is it?"

Ariel smiled. "Come and see," he said.

When I arrived at his apartment the next afternoon, I was unprepared for what I saw. Welcoming me into the dark, crowded living room, Jordan stood in the midst of a mess of the most nightmarish paintings, sculptures, and photo collages I had ever seen in my life, a virtual horror show of the psyche. There were images of naked men and women in cartoon masks, holding children like sacrifices between them; there were photos of grotesque body parts—penises, vaginas, shrieking mouths—overlaid with domestic scenes, framed in bolted steel with combinations of words around the borders: LOVE DESTRUCTION TYRANNY SEX. There were ritualistic tribal masks, hallucinatory appliqués of infants crawling across canvases covered with worms and tortured primary colors. As I stood there silently taking these images in, Jordan picked up something from the floor and handed it to me. It was a papier mâché baby doll whose body had been covered with orifices, gashes, and pricks, its mouth a gaping red vagina, open lipped as if howling in violation.

"My God," I said, holding the doll, "what is this?"

"It's my healing," said Ariel Jordan.

"It's disgusting."

"Do you really think so?" He seemed genuinely surprised by my reaction.

"Sorry," I said. "But yes."

"I don't mind," Ariel said. Then he poured me a cup of coffee and told me his story.

He was born on a kibbutz in the upper Galilee, where his mother and father were pillars of the community. When he was four, his father raped him for the first time. "He had given me a bath and it felt so good, because my parents rarely touched me," Ariel explained. "I worshiped my father. I remember him drying me off, tickling me. It was wonderful until he started to stick his tongue in my mouth. He seemed to be in a kind of trance, and when he penetrated me from behind, the pain was so excruciating that part of me died." Ariel reported all this without drama in his voice, or self-pity. "This went on until I was fifteen."

"What about your mother?" I asked.

"She looked the other way. Sometimes they would take me to their bed and have sex with me together. Do you know what it's like for a teenage boy to have intercourse with his mother?"

I shook my head, too stunned to speak. My impulse was to stand up, leave the apartment, and never speak to Ariel Jordan again. Until that moment, I had not believed that such things as Ariel was describing actually happened. This was years before the Menendez brothers, before it was hip to be abused; incest was a primitive crime, I imagined, like cannibalism, and just as rare; besides, stories were easy to make up or exaggerate. But pain was not: the agony I felt screaming from Ariel Jordan's artwork could not be faked. Listening to him describe the awful crimes of his family, committed just behind the screen of the "normal" world, I realized (as I had in Thalheim) that here was another, parallel universe, requiring a leap of faith to apprehend. Just as Mother Meera had been a door to the light, I sensed that Ariel Jordan might be a door to the darkness, an underworld where horror happened on a regular basis. Just as I had scrutinized Mother Meera for signs that she was not holy and that the mystical dimension she pointed to was a fantasy, so I studied Ariel Jordan with that same scrupulousness for signs of fakery. I found none.

"Why are you telling me this?" I asked.

"You're on a spiritual journey, aren't you?"

"Yes."

"This is important information. Most survivors become seekers. They have to in order to survive." He paused. "The minute a child is raped, he loses his parents and becomes an orphan. His entire system goes bankrupt and he learns to function as a fake, an impostor. This creates enormous existential pain that seeks comfort wherever it can. That's why victims have such an unusual capacity for transcendence. I remember when I was six years old, looking at the sun shining on the wall, seeing the light flicker on the stone, feeling the breeze on my arm, and realizing that *something* out there loved me. That was the only thing that kept me going. Most survivors have intense skin hunger—we learn to take whatever nurturing we can from anything, no matter how small. Like a cactus in the desert." When Ariel said this, he looked me squarely in the eye.

"I know the feeling," I said.

"I thought you would," he said. "I work with survivors. I've learned to read the signs."

"You think I'm a survivor of *incest?*" I asked, more shocked than offended.

Ariel watched me carefully, with eyes that were deep and soft and brown.

Though I'd never thought of myself as an incest survivor, I could not deny that the fractured emotional landscape Ariel was describing did mirror my own inner life. Still, I wasn't at all sure I was ready to be a member of this club or to label myself in this extreme way.

"I think I'd better go now," I said, rising to get my coat. At the door I turned to look around the room again at the nightmare images, framed and strewn all over the floor. "But I'll be back."

For days afterward, the images of that artwork wouldn't leave me, especially the terrible doll. When I closed my eyes, I saw the gaping red mouth of the papier mâché fuck baby and wanted to scream myself. That doll had made me remember things—things I'd never really forgotten but that now, brought back by Ariel's story, returned to me more vividly, faded images suddenly come back to life.

My mother is lying in the bathtub looking at me. Her short dark hair is brushed dykishly off her face, her huge breasts hanging to her abdomen and slipping off to the side like bags of wet cement, the nipples dark and bigger than my hand. As she watches me, she brings the cigarette to her mouth, sucks hard, closes her eyes, exhales slowly.

I sit on the john and watch my mother smoke, waiting for the sign that she's ready for me. When the cigarette's practically burning her fingers, she tosses it in the toilet and says, "All right, kiddo, your turn."

I slip out of my shorts and shirt, and lower myself between my mother's legs, toboggan style. It feels weird, but good to be here. This is as close as I ever get to her, here in our private place—the only place where my mother touches me. Ida doesn't kiss or hug—she doesn't want a mama's boy—but behind the locked bathroom door on quiet afternoons, when the girls are at school and I'm playing hooky, we can have our time together.

My mother clutches me between her knees and pushes her pussy against me. I can feel the scratchy hair on my backbone, the warm lips suctioning my skin through the tepid water. My mother's breasts are pressed against my shoulder blades, and turning my face toward her, I can smell tobacco and the damp perfume of her skin. As she holds me, I gaze up over heads at the yellowed tile and the brown panty hose hanging from the shower like phantom legs.

"Wash me," I say, but I don't have to ask. Sooner or later, my mother will take the nub of soap from the dish and slide it down my torso, around my belly button, down my legs and inside my thighs, lingering in the crease above my butt until it tickles. Then she will take my penis, no bigger than her pinky, and hold it between her fingers, gently pulling on the tip while I watch her. As she pulls, she'll hum, and when I begin to get an erection, my mother will hoot with mock surprise. "Look at that little weenie!" she says, flipping my boner from side to side, laughing. "Let's hope they didn't cut off too much." When I was eight days old, I was strapped to a breadboard on my aunt Ruthie's kitchen table and circumcised by an Orthodox rabbi. My mother never tired of telling the story: how my father fainted when he saw the blood—how she screamed at the rabbi that he'd cut off too much. Now she examines me for herself and seems satisfied. "I think you're gonna be all right," she says, stroking from the base to the head. "Like your son of a bitch father." When I feel like I'm gonna pee, I squirm and tell her to let me go, but my mother locks her knees together until finally I stop resisting. Our ritual continues, off and on, until I'm seven.

Even when I was small, I knew that there was something wrong with this picture. Other memories troubled me as well: the way my mother flaunted herself in front of me in her baby doll nightie; the soft-core *True Confessions* magazines she left on the coffee table for all of us to see; the tales she told me about my father's virility. Troubling as these lapses were, however, they seemed to be in the natural order of things as well, since nothing was quite appropriate or normal in our house. The question now was whether or not my mother's loose behavior was actually incest.

In the weeks that followed, I explored this question with Ariel, lying on a thick foam pad in the soundproofed office where he worked. Recalling these memories and others, hesitating to call them by their rightful name, Ariel encouraged me to tell the truth, to stop reflexively excusing these violations. Each time I reminded him how lonely Ida had been, how certain I was that she meant no harm, how she herself had been sexually wounded, how much she loved me, he waved my rationalizations aside. "When a blind man steps on your foot, it still hurts," he insisted.

As our sessions progressed, Ariel helped me to understand that the disjointed, orphaned feeling I'd had since childhood was not unfounded. There was a *reason* that half of me always felt like it was in shadow, ghostly, unreal. There was a reason that I saw myself as split in two: half alive, half dead, half boy, half girl, half dark, half light, half here, half gone. There was a reason why, underneath the mask I showed the world, I felt inexplicably evil, as though I'd done something terrible without knowing what or when or why. Something had indeed happened in our house to create these feelings of shame, feelings long trapped inside my body.

During one of our sessions, Ariel showed me a photograph of

himself when he was four years old, standing with his father. The boy's face was stunned, scared, as if he'd just stopped shrieking. By creepy contrast, his father's face was relaxed and smiling—he was a handsome man with wavy, dark hair, deep-set eyes, a marked cleft in the middle of his chin. His face conjured up another time, and staring into the image, I journeyed back to another morning, twenty-five years before this one.

My father had a cleft, too, a deep one like Kirk Douglas. On the day that now came back to me, I am standing close to him under steaming water in the shower. It's early in the morning, and in front of my face, his long penis is streaming with water, thick and flesh brown like the cow's tongue my mother brings home from the deli. I want to bite my father's cock, it looks so delicious, like sandwich meat. But I'm afraid to. Instead, I reach out and give it a squeeze.

He pushes my hand away. I grab the head of his cock again, and pull it hard.

"Ouch! Hey, easy," he says. Then he turns the bar of soap in his hands and slowly lathers up his dick, stroking from the bottom, stretching the full length of it, then tickling the vein underneath. I watch in awe through the pounding water as my father's cock rises inch by inch.

I lean forward and kiss it.

"Hey, cut that out," my father whispers, pulling my face aside, against his hip. I've never been so happy in my life, never before felt so scared or excited as this before, with my father's hand pulling my face against his body, the hot water pounding over us, binding us together, away from the girls, away from my mother; just me and my father, wet and naked.

I reach out again and touch the head of my father's cock. At that second, he lets out a long groan and grabs me around the ribs, digging his fingers in, tickling me till I fall down on the shower floor, squirming and screaming and laughing. This brings my mother running. "What's going on in there?" she shouts through the locked door.

My father puts his finger to his lips. "Nothing!" he yells back. The game is over.

Afterward, I stand in front of the wall heater while my father wraps me in a thick white towel and dries me from head to toe, rubbing my hair with his hands. I sit on the toilet and watch him shave, twirling the brush in the soap dish, painting the foam on his cheeks and neck. I put my feet on top of his and sit there gazing up at him, adoring him as he hums and runs the razor through the creamy white. Then he cuts himself as usual, curses, wads up a piece of toilet paper, and sticks it to the blood in the cleft of his chin.

"Mark?" Ariel's voice interrupted my reverie. "Where did you go?"

I looked at Ariel sitting across from me, holding the photograph, and described in detail the scene I'd just remembered. Did this qualify as sexual assault, or was my father's little show just a form of paternal bonding? Ariel immediately set me straight.

"In houses where boundaries don't exist, the degree of sexual trauma is not necessarily in proportion to the act itself," he explained. In other words, tempting as it might be to downplay the events of my own childhood next to horror stories like Ariel's, such thinking was self-deceptive. Invisible rapes could be as devastating as physical penetration, he said, sometimes more so, since these acts masqueraded as love. Ariel explained to me that a father giving his daughter sexy lingerie might be worse in certain cases than if he'd actually climbed on top of her. It was the *degree* of sexualization—the shock and impact rather than the details—that constituted rape.

Leaving Ariel's basement and walking down Broadway, I

considered the possibility that, in their own ways, both of my parents had raped me. Oddly, the thought came as a relief. Somehow, with the facts on the table, the memories that had lingered hidden and abstract in my psyche no longer seemed so threatening. The wound that had always seemed so *enormous* suddenly came down to scale, and a darkness I'd never understood began to fade in the light of awareness.

Despite the sadness these memories evoked, I bounded down the street, feeling inexplicably happy. I'd rather be sad than numb, I was thinking—better shaken up than paralyzed. Perhaps I could learn to love after all, with body, mind, and spirit joined together. Perhaps I could learn to trust this beast inside me that had caused me so much trouble; or maybe, I ventured, it wasn't a beast at all, but just a boy craving to be touched.

I reported all this to Alexander on the phone, telling him about Ariel Jordan and the dark memories coming back to me. He sounded pleased. "It's part of the game," Alexander said. "Every time you get a little light, you have to use it to go deeper into the darkness. It's a simultaneous ascent and descent. But be careful."

"Of what?" I asked.

"Not getting stuck there. It's like exploring a pit. You can either jump down inside it and risk getting sucked in, or you can lean over the side with a flashlight and examine the darkness from above." As he said this, I understood that if I had not glimpsed the light of holy love in Mother Meera, I would not now be seeing the shadow so clearly.

Ariel had once said to me, "A human being is like a cup. Until you grieve and empty the cup, nothing new can fill it."

This is what was happening now: I was finally grieving—not diving into the hole but examining it—and as I did, weeping for what was lost there, making room, I hoped, for something new to finally enter in.

FIFTEEN

I BROKE MY celibacy after eight months, with a boy I'd slept with casually before. He came to my house with a bottle of red wine, and after we'd both loosened up, I attempted to make love to him. It was a disastrous half hour of fervid squirming and apologies; no matter how hard I tried to concentrate on the physical act, my body would not cooperate. The harder I tried, the softer I got, until I gave up completely. This was not only humiliating but frightening. I had meant my experiment in celibacy to lead to higher consciousness, not impotence.

The boy, who'd known me years before as a self-proclaimed stud, was surprised, not offended, when I talked about my feelings, trying to create a bridge of intimacy between us.

"I have skid marks from one end of me to the other," he told me, referring to his own love life. This confession only made me want to comfort him, protect him, care for him. I could not respond to him as meat, and we ended up having a long talk about what was missing from his life and how his spirit had been damaged.

"You know, you're different," the boy said, studying me as he was dressing. "You used to be hotter. But I like you more now."

Though celibacy had turned out to be easier than I expected—so easy, in fact, that I found myself forgetting about sex for weeks at a time—this honeymoon with myself couldn't last indefinitely. I had no intention of living as a monk, and abstinence was not a long-term solution. It wasn't enough to lock the beast up and pretend that it had been transformed; I needed to find a way to open the door and feed the thing, without it biting my hand off. I was wary of becoming a hypocrite, or a repressed fanatic, like a priest twirling his rosary beads faster and faster to keep images of altar boys away. I didn't want to use philosophy to build a prison for myself, or confuse spirituality with a false morality. After seven months without having sex, it was time to find the balance between celibacy and promiscuity, desire and obsession.

I'd had moments of this balance during my abstinence. For several months, with the prospect of sex removed, I had begun to know my body and the bodies of other people quite differently, with an innocence and playfulness that lust had made impossible. For the first time ever, I could actually walk through the streets of New York City on a hot summer day, surrounded by shirtless men in Calvin Klein boxer shorts, smooth-legged girls in tight skirts, and delight in their beauty without the compulsion to fuck them. My style began to change too. I was no longer moving like a predator, I realized, stalking, chasing, one eye over my shoulder. I was no longer feeling male in that old rutting macho way, and with this animal thing toned down, an androgynous feeling arose in me—not neutered, but sensual, hyperaware of sights, smells, sensations that I hadn't noticed before: a whole range of erotic possibilities that my fixation with conquest had dulled, I was like someone who quits smoking and can suddenly taste things.

Best of all, I felt a softening in my heart, a deeper affection for myself and for the people around me, as if a callus were dissolving.

It was this new sense of openness that I wanted to share, despite my lackluster maiden voyage with the boy who brought the red wine.

But breaking my celibacy also meant that I couldn't keep putting off the HIV test indefinitely.

"How can you say that you're willing to face your fear if you're not willing to get the information?" a friend asked me. "It's all well and good to talk about saints, but if you're afraid of a little blood test, it's all a crock of shit."

He was referring to Ramana Maharshi, whose story of enlightenment through the fear of death I had just been sharing. The maharshi, one of India's greatest saints of the modern age, had been an ordinary teenage boy when, one day in his sixteenth year, alone in his mother's house, he was overwhelmed by the awareness that he would die. Rather than run away from this terror, he went straight into it, lay down on the floor like a corpse, and stopped breathing. He thought, *This body will die and be carted off to the cremation grounds, and so, what then?* At that moment paralyzed by fear, Ramana Maharshi reported that an extraordinary liberation occurred. He realized, with visceral clarity, that he was *not* that body. He realized, through the process of elimination, that far from being this "thing" that would die, he was, in essence, the witness beyond it, the pure observing spirit.

Inspired by Ramana Maharshi, I knew that sooner or later I would have to stare down my own terror. I scheduled an appointment for the HIV test on March 30, 1989. I was casual about it with friends, who warned me against my usual bravado.

"Look," I said to Robert, "I've been living as *if* for so long that it won't be a surprise. Nothing will change, it's just a formality. I'm doing it to be responsible."

"Be prepared," said Robert, who was working extensively with people with AIDS. "You think you're prepared, but it sneaks up on you." Robert was, in fact, too frightened to take the test himself. "Formalities change lives," he said. "It's the difference between dating and getting married. Except with HIV there's no divorce."

I felt nothing. Some moments are too big to be felt, except in retrospect. I felt nothing at all when the nervous Puerto Rican drew my blood at the clinic on Ninth Avenue. We chatted about my sex life: who fucked whom how often, sheathed in what. I answered him that I undoubtedly had the virus and probably had since I was sixteen years old, long before Patient Zero came up sick; I'd had a strange case of thrush and shingles together, to our family doctor's complete confusion. Now, I told the man in the white coat that I was not afraid.

For the next two weeks, I practically forgot about the test. When I returned for my results and the kindly technician informed me that the antibodies of the virus that might or might not kill me were indeed present in my blood (which otherwise was normal), I felt nothing. He began to list my options and recommendations for safe sex. I reached across the desk, patted his hand, and told him not to bother, that I was well aware of the data, and was he all right? He looked so sad.

"There are so many of you," he said, relegating me to the herd, as if HIV had, in that second, become my new identity.

My worst fear was telling my mother. I had morbid fantasies about Ida walking into my sickroom and seeing me for the first time after a major bout of something, the look of fear and pity on her face. The thought of Ida's pain terrified me more than my own; it never occurred to me that my mother's presence might be a comfort in my illness. Thinking of my mother watching me die only filled me with dread.

When I finally told her on the telephone, a year later, Ida said: "No child of mine will ever have to die alone." It moved me to hear her say this, though I knew it wasn't true—at least it hadn't been for Marcia.

"Thanks, Mom," I said. "But I'm asymptomatic."

"What does that mean?"

"I'll let you know if I ever need you."

She rarely brought up the subject again.

I tried to convince myself that nothing had changed, but in the weeks following my diagnosis, I veered between terror, numbness, and the sense of this as a holy opportunity. In an effort to strengthen my immunity, I decided to turn to a strict macrobiotic diet. For eight months, I lived on rice, gluten, greens, and various sea vegetables guaranteed to cleanse my blood, increase my energy, and make me a better person. For eight months, I was bloated, spending every free minute counting leaves of *kombu*, drinking *amazake*, skinning burdock, and chopping *mochi*. Determined to cultivate my T-cells with brown rice, to ward off the enemy with *hijiki*, not a day passed that I did not stuff myself with grains. I tried to muster a certain reverence as I boiled quinoa ("grain of the Incas!") and looked down my nose at people who drank tap water. My inner hygiene became a mission, and I intended to turn a lifetime of greasy eating habits into a yoga of perfect consumption.

As part of this strict regimen to purify and strengthen our bodies, Carole and I visited a holistic practitioner, who supplemented the macrobiotic diet with a few items of his own, including a breakfast drink of raw calf's liver and carrot juice, run through a blender, and enemas self-administered three times daily to cleanse the colon of toxins.

"I'm in my bathroom period," I told my friends. When I wasn't by the sink trying not to choke up the orange mess in the morning, I was staring at my feet propped up on the bathtub tiles while the contents of a half-gallon rubber bag flowed into my rectum.

In the end, the only alteration in my mental state was an increased mean-spiritedness, due to constant, nagging hunger. I looked at the other macrobiotics around me, bony scarecrows with resigned smiles, and thought, do I want to look like them? Once, the chef at an East Village macro place I frequented—the thinnest person I had ever seen outside a hospital—keeled over into the turnip greens and *kuki-cha* tea and died of no apparent cause. As the pounds dripped off me, people started to look at me strangely on the street, as if I were one of *them*. I needed a burger fast.

One day I found a quarter-sized lump in my neck, two inches below my ear. Dr. Weissman told me it was lymphadenopathy—swollen glands—an early sign of infection. The other larger lump in my armpit was still there. When he palpated this one, the side of his mouth twitched.

"ARC," he said, as if it were nothing. "AIDS-related complex."

I left Weissman's office in a morbid daze and sat on a bench in Washington Square, staring at the people walking by as if I were already dead. I thought, this bench will be empty soon. I'll go from present tense to past tense, but nothing else will change; the children will still be playing on the swings, the crazy man with the Sherlock Holmes cap and pipe will still be sitting in his tweeds, arguing with himself; the pushers will still be hawking nickel bags of pot; the leaves will fall again in November and return in April. Nothing will change, only I won't be here; my head will sink below the surface, life will close down over me, and in an instant my ripple on the surface of this world will disappear. I sat there in the park, feeling my neck with one hand, my armpit with the other.

In fearful times, everything became a symptom. I had always enjoyed looking in the mirror; now I sidled up to it full of dread. Every morning I was scared I'd find a lesion on my face. I held my breath and opened my mouth, sure that my tongue would be covered with sores or trush. I looked into my eyes for signs of the CMV that could blind me. I brushed my teeth and, when I *hocked*, examined the color of the sputum in the sink. Sitting on the can, I wondered whether the cold on my bare feet against the tile floor was normal cold or the tingly numb cold of neuropathy. Before I flushed, I examined the turds for looseness, hardness, mucus, parasites. In the shower, I examined every inch of my skin for irregularities, my groin for swollen glands, my toenails for fungus, trying desperately to turn this terrifying sequence into a relaxed, normal routine.

I sat on a folding chair in a loft in SoHo, waiting with twenty other people to be examined by Dr. Choedak, the ex-personal physician to the Dalai Lama. He was in New York to see people with the virus in hopes that the Tibetan system could help where Western drugs had failed. My stomach was in knots—all doctors make me extremely nervous—but the prospect of being examined by someone with developed intuitive powers as well as medical expertise was even worse. I watched the seventy-year-old man in an ocher monk's robe as he diagnosed the people in front of me, then tried to calm myself by meditating on the Tibetan *tangkas*—traditional religious paintings on silk—hanging on either side of the examination area.

When my turn came, I sat before Dr. Choedak, who asked me questions through a young translator-nun. When he touched my wrist to take my pulses (the Tibetans determine the condition of various internal organs by their corresponding pulse), I was surprised by how soft and gentle his hands were, like a baby's, except for the scars where he was tortured by the Chinese during twenty years in prison. He saw me looking at his hands and smiled, then indicated that I should stick out my tongue. I held my breath in fear of what he might see. Then he looked into my eyes and said something in Tibetan to the translator. She looked at me and said, "Not strong."

Cold sweat dropped down my forehead. "What do you mean, not strong?" I asked.

The nun asked Dr. Choedak for an explanation. He talked for a minute, pointing now and then at different parts of my body.

She turned to me and smiled. "Virus not strong," she said.

I locked myself in the bathroom and cried.

The terror burned me, caught me off guard, made everything urgent. It also pushed me on the spiritual path. I was grasping for answers as a way to save my life—if not my body—something to hold on to as the water slipped over my head.

My terror held me to God. Every onslaught of fear showed me this more deeply. In my journal, I wrote:

> Terror is the door to enlightenment. Crisis takes you to the brink and forces you to keep moving or die of fear. When people in crisis say things like "illness is a blessing," they're describing this paradox. It's why men love war, why women love childbirth: because on that knife blade of danger and pain they come alive as never before. There's a vitality in facing death, a rush that comes from knowing it, smelling it, feeling its shadow engulf you. It pushes you to travel fast and

deep and wide; it expands the heart and brings up reserves of courage you didn't know you had, like adrenaline in the muscles of a mother saving her child. Only *you* are the child, and it's your life, the life of your own soul, that you are saving.

SIXTEEN

ALTHOUGH I WAS doing my best to use my fear as grist for the mill, much of my life in New York seemed to contradict my experiences in Thalheim and India. Often I was plagued by doubt and the trashy old pull of New York hype. Arriving home one day after a scary meeting with an agent who thought I was "absolutely perfect" to ghostwrite the spiritual autobiography of Shirley MacLaine, I found a short note from Alexander, with the following quotation from Satprem scribbled in his chicken-scratch hand:

Remember the dark half of the truth. The seeker began his journey with a positive experience. He felt a new vibration which made life clearer, more alive. The sign may come in a thousand ways that a new rhythm is setting in. Then, after this hopeful start, everything becomes veiled, as if he had been dreaming or even carried away by a somewhat childish enthusiasm. Something in him is busy taking its revenge through a spell of skepticism, disgust and revolt. That will be the second sign, perhaps the true one, that he is progressing.

Perhaps instead of being the sign of failure I took it for, my doubt was serving a real purpose, testing me, purifying my aspiration, forcing me to choose again the mystery over the old cynical mind.

*

The writing gig with Joe kept me going. I did interviews with authors, some by phone, some in person. I told myself that this was a respectable compromise between prostitution and high-mindedness—a sort of journalistic middle path for the seeker with a rent to pay. Joe was saintly in his assignments and loose in his deadlines. I spoke to Anne Rice about the relationship between the bloodsucking orgies of her vampire heroes and her fictional taste for S&M. I spoke to Peter Matthiessen about his twenty-five years of Zen practice and the disappearing American wilderness. I spent an afternoon with Kurt Vonnegut—who looked like an antediluvian surfer exhumed from some primordial beach—talking about the future of the world.

"You want to know why nobody wants to save the planet?" Vonnegut asked me at his kitchen table.

"They don't know how," I said.

"Bullshit," he said, lowering his reading glasses onto his nose and fixing me with his big sad bug eyes. "The reason nobody wants to save the planet is that they're all so fucking depressed they really don't *care* if life goes on or not."

I thought about this when I left Vonnegut's apartment. Was it true? I didn't think so; nor did I want to be part of the propaganda machine that perpetuated such visionless despair. The world *was* in a sorry state, but cawing over hopelessness like a crow over a dung heap was not the appropriate response. This was the self-satisfied nihilism that had set me running from New York in the first place, and hearing it again now, out of the mouth of such an intelligent, gifted man, only reminded me of who I wasn't, what I didn't think, what I didn't want to write about for a living. I told this to Joe, who agreed but could do nothing to coerce his editor in chief into opening the pages of *Harper's Bazaar* to more enlightening subjects. Rather than waste my time pounding on the doors of the mainstream media, screaming, *Open up, you need a revelation!* I decided to turn to smaller magazines that embraced the journalism of consciousness and were more than happy to assign me stories that genuinely interested me. The first of these was for *Common Boundary*, which commissioned a cover story on Stephen Levine and his wife, Ondrea.

I'd wanted to meet the Levines for years. It was Stephen's books—*Who Dies?* and *Meetings at the Edge*—that I'd found sitting on Bob's bedside table as he was dying. It was Levine who called every few days from his mountain retreat in New Mexico to walk Bob through his pain and fear, tell him dharma stories, and make him laugh.

The day before my interview with the Levines was scheduled, I went with Carole—and four hundred other people—to their workshop on death and spirituality. Ondrea, in leotards and a wraparound skirt, looked like an aerobics teacher; Stephen, in a T-shirt and Birkenstocks, was tousled and teddy-bearish with a white beard and curly hair. They sat in chairs at center stage, separated by an arrangement of flowers. Ondrea folded her legs and closed her eyes.

"When you work with as many people as we do," Levine said, "you really get to see how permeable the boundary between life and death is. Tell me, how many of you have had visitations from people who've died?" I raised my hand, along with more than half the people in the auditorium.

Shortly before leaving New York for India, I had had what could only be called a visitation by my sister Marcia. The experience was three-dimensional, with a completely different texture and feel than a dream. It felt distinctly real: There was a knock on the door. I opened it and saw Marcia, radiant and smiling, standing next to a tall man I didn't recognize. She put her arms around my neck and pulled me to her, whispering in my ear, "I'm fine." It was *her* voice, *her* body, the unmistakable smell of her breath.

I'd woken suddenly, overcome with happiness and the conviction that this had been a direct communication. Marcia's death was the bloodstain our family couldn't wash off; the memory that stood to remind us of what we had not loved enough. I was the one who knew this best, so it was easy to understand why Marcia had come to me, to tell me what I already knew: that she was better off where she was, that she had, in actuality, saved her own life by dying.

"Once you see enough people die and come back to life, descend into a coma and return, or journey to the other side in trance or meditation," Levine continued, "you begin to see that the states we call 'life' and 'death' are phases on a continuum that are constantly bleeding into each other. There is so much to learn and nothing to fear.

"How many of you have had near-death experiences?" Several dozen people raised their hands. "You saw the big white light, but what you may not have realized is that this light is not something outside yourself. It is your own original nature, your Great Nature.

"Let me tell you a story about a woman who came to us," Levine continued. "Her ten-year-old daughter had disappeared while she was swimming. A few days later, the mother was called to identify what was left of her daughter's body at the morgue. She went completely out of her mind with grief, but when her heart broke open, she was transformed. Her own agony left her exposed to the agony of the world. She realized that it wasn't just her pain—it was *the* pain, the communal pain—and this opened her to other people. When she told me her story, I said that horrible as this accident was, grace had, in fact, come to her in the form of a shark."

Savage grace, I thought.

"Whatever it takes to break your heart and wake you up is grace."

"Mark?" I turned around and saw a man I barely recognized looking at me. I had slept with him once. The last time I'd seen him, he looked like Antonio Banderas. Now David wore a scarf around his head, weighed a hundred pounds, and had no eyebrows.

AIDS was doing strange things to time and memory, making things surreal, fractured, grotesque. Sometimes I couldn't remember if people were alive or dead. Once you heard they were sick, they were already dead in your mind. In the face of so much illness, you couldn't quite place who was at what point on the line of disappearing. One day you'd see a boy sweating and gorgeous, bulging in his bicycle shorts as he sped up Sixth Avenue, winking as he passed. The next, you'd see him, pale and ghostly, dragging himself up a ramp at GMHC with a cane, another person entirely, no middle point, just a fast-forward meltdown, non sequitur frames with nothing in between. Everywhere you turned, people were leaking out of themselves, leaving their chrysalis behind them, frail and light as dust on the sidewalks of New York.

Looking at David now after so long, I thought: the dying have eyes on both sides of their heads, feet pointing in two directions. His face was positively serene.

"Levine's the only one who really gets it," said David. "He gets the meditation part and the death part. And he's not flaky." It was true that there seemed to be nothing flaky about Stephen Levine. Once a ten-year-old has died of leukemia in your arms; once the hundredth man consumed by AIDS has vomited on your shoulder; once a ninety-year-old has called you in the middle of the night to tell you that she can't die because she's afraid of being eaten by worms; once death has seeped so deeply into your heart that you wear it as a badge, a pass of entry into any stranger's grief, it's difficult to be flaky. Dying wears you away. Levine reminded me of an old blanket a thousand people had wrapped around themselves. He was weary, warm, wise, and as humane as any man I'd ever listened to. I already loved him.

The next morning, I met the Levines in their hotel room. Stephen sat on the couch rolling a cigarette. Ondrea was in the midst of packing. We talked about Bob.

"An extraordinary guy," said Stephen. "He died with such style and spirit.

"If spiritual growth can be defined as the accumulation of insight and the opening of the heart," Stephen continued, "then there's no place on the planet—no monastery in Dharmasala, Poona, or Peru—where growth is happening more rapidly than in the AIDS community. It's the leading edge of spiritual growth in the world today. Nowhere can we learn more about the power of love. People who are dying themselves are sitting at each other's bedsides. I know no parallel to that."

This was a startling remark, reminding me that one of the unique things about this virus—terrible as it is—was that it killed its victims so slowly, allowing us ten, sometimes fifteen years after the diagnosis to make significant changes of heart and mind, while those afflicted with other diseases were not often afforded this opportunity.

There was no question that the sound of the bomb ticking inside my body had set my inner journey in motion, urging me to wonder about what was *not* the body and why I was in the world in the first place. No matter how I wanted the disease gone and the epidemic over, I could not deny the good that had come from my infection: I could not be anything but grateful, though words like *gratitude* sound too simple. I was grateful, yes, and angry, too, not to mention

170

sad, frightened, and strangely released. I was learning that responses to fate's extreme truths are necessarily complex; that the worst times are sometimes also the best; that beauty can root in the ugliest misfortune, like the "garbage trees" in Manhattan that grow in undumped cans, creating an odor both musty and green.

I took Stephen Levine's remark as my precept for surviving this disease—or living with it at least—for witnessing the grief around me without feeling swamped or hopeless. If it was true that there was another face to this epidemic, like the secret Buddhas hidden at the back of dark Indian temples; if, instead of mere horror, this plague contained the seeds of transformation; if this *were* so, and suffering was, indeed, a *redemptive* experience, then the whole cynical view exploded, taking depression and bitterness with it.

I could see this redemption in the lives around me. People who didn't give a damn about spirituality before their lives fell apart were now having intensive awakening experiences. Often these skeptics hadn't found God but *had* found love. Often they hadn't gone out questing, but instead they had stayed right where they were, in ailing bodies, and learned more than many more adventurous seekers I knew. This reminded me of Augustine's remark that when a thing is everywhere, the way to find it is not to travel but to love.

Now that I knew for certain that I had HIV, the fundamental question was how to live, how to settle in for the long haul. The answer was paradoxical: I had to live as if my body mattered, realizing that ultimately it did not; to live as if I might be alive in twenty years, knowing that I might not be; to follow the middle path between opposites; to rest at the still point which does not waver while moving forward.

On the subway downtown after saying good-bye to the Levines,

I ran into the ad girl from *Interview*. She looked up from her copy of *Women's Wear Daily*, stared at me, and squinted. She didn't recognize me until I said, "Diana?"

"Is that *you?*" she screamed. "What did you do to your hair?"

"I shaved it."

"Cool." She crossed the train and kissed me on both cheeks, then ran her finger over the stubble on my head. "Like Mahatma Gandhi. I can't believe it's you. Hey, didn't you go to India?"

I nodded.

"Wow. so what are you, like, enlightened now?" she asked, putting her hand on her hip.

"Completely."

"Come on."

"I'm not."

"Then why did you go?"

"Because it was there."

"*Puhleez.*" Diana was still sassy, still chewed her gum like Shirley MacLaine in *Irma la Douce*. "You know, you always were a brat. And you want to know what else?"

"Tell me."

Diana laughed. "Everybody thought you were dead."

"That's nice."

"We thought you went to India because you were dying. Isn't that bizarre?"

Just then, the train pulled into the Christopher Street station. "Hey, it was great to see you," Diana yelled over the conductor's voice, pressing a business card into my hand. "You look good. Bald, but good."

"You too."

She bustled off toward the exit. At the bottom of the stairs, she turned and looked me up and down again. "You *sure* you're not enlightened?" she asked.

"Positive."

"What a waste," she said. "You were a really good editor."

SEVENTEEN

DEAN REYNOLDS CAME floating into the café, looking like an insect in big glasses, a yellow bandanna wrapped around his head. If I hadn't already heard that Dean was a long-term survivor of AIDS, I would never have guessed it. His age was unclear, but what I couldn't mistake was the quality of his energy, festive, gossipy, amused. I liked Dean Reynolds at once.

"Honey, those Zen Buddhists are a bunch of drips," he said, patting my hand and following the waiters' buttocks with his eyes as they flexed past him toward the kitchen.

"Are they really?"

"Ghouls, my dear," Dean assured me. "So judgmental, so serious. I've gone past them now."

Dean told me his story. He had been a Wall Street banker and art maven in New York, a smart-boy party animal, hanging with Andy Warhol and his cronies, making buckets of money and generally running himself into the ground.

"I couldn't stop," he said. "I was spinning, spinning, too much to do and all of it so *exciting*. I mean, who in his right mind would stay home when Andy called? Who'd stay sober when you could do lines and watch the strippers at 54? I was young, I was hot, I was loaded. It was like being at one long fabulous party. But you know what those parties are like at five A.M., when half the people have passed out, the place stinks, the sun's coming up, and you just can't face it? Well, my life started to feel like five A.M. The music stopped, and there I was, burned out, hung over, completely lost. I needed an excuse to get out. So I got sick."

"On purpose?"

"That's a complex question. Did I get fucked by somebody who was sick on purpose? No. I just got fucked by everybody. But there was a definite connection between my burning out, my needing a reason to leave New York, my emptiness—and my disease. Without question. I got my first lesion on a Thursday, gave notice on a Friday, and moved to a monastery near San Francisco two weeks later. That was five years ago, and it's keeping me alive."

"The monastery?"

"Being free, being away from that world, having permission to live the way I want to live. This disease has been my savior."

"Most people don't buy that," I said, thinking of the patronizing looks I'd gotten when I suggested that this virus had actually saved my life.

"They're scared. It's too much for them to take in. I've seen street kids—I mean real scum-bucket hustlers—come to the hospice with AIDS and turn their lives around. One of them was ordained as a priest a couple of months before he died. This is the fast track to enlightenment, honey."

"Tell me."

"Not that I'm enlightened," Dean continued, "but the fact that I'm sitting here proves something. I was supposed to be dead three years ago. My numbers say I shouldn't be alive. It's almost embarrassing when I go to my doctors now. It's like, 'Sorry I'm proving you wrong,' but the fact of the matter is that they don't know a goddamn thing about what the spirit can do."

"How do you explain it?"

"Little pops," said Dean, snapping his fingers. "Satoris—like something popping in your brain. When I'm least expecting it, not on the *zafu* necessarily—but on a bus, in the hospital, even when I'm sleeping—there are these little snaps when everything comes together and I feel incredibly light. Suddenly, in those moments, I can see it."

"What?"

"The world as it *really* is. I see love in people's faces, even when there's pain. Your heart breaks and something unbelievably sweet comes out. Everything seems luminous." Dean cut himself short.

"Please," I encouraged, transported by what he was saying.

"When it comes, I can actually see that life is a *rapture*. All of it, even the torment. But words can't really capture the feeling." Dean took a packet of pills from his pocket and swallowed them. "Unfortunately," he continued, "the Buddhists were not amused by me. As soon as I started wanting to venture out, let loose, *live* a little, the axe came down. But when you know you're going to die, you don't care about that dogmatic shit. You're looking at something so much bigger. It's not a hobby; it's a matter of life and death."

"My therapist used to say that when you really see how dangerous life is, you find your way to spiritual practice like a cockroach finds a crack," I said.

"But when your disease becomes your practice, it's even better," said Dean. "Take it from me, I've been pricked and prodded and bled and hosed out from one end of this body to the other. There isn't a hole they haven't pumped or an inch of skin they haven't zapped with radioactivity. But I swear on everything I know and love that it's those satori moments, those little snaps of bliss, that are keeping me alive. My Buddhist friends say it's just more illusion, more attachment, but I love those moments more than anything I've loved in my lifetime, and if it's wrong to be attached to them, well tough! The heart can't survive without hope."

"Even when what you hope for isn't possible?"

"Hope doesn't need an object. Hope is a feeling; it says the world will continue, whether I'm in this body or not. You know the painting of 'Hope' in the Tate Gallery?"

"A blindfolded woman playing a harp with one string."

"Yes," he answered. "And do you know why she plays?"

"Because she'd be a fool not to?"

"Exactly," said Dean.

The terror brought on by the knowledge of the virus circulating in my bloodstream came in waves. I would ignore it for as long as possible, then it would catch up with me, crowding everything else out of my mind, forcing me to look at it squarely. Any attempt to avoid the anxiety only made it worse. I knew I had to go through it, not around or over it—straight through—to really *feel* the sensation of panic in my body—and let the virus become my teacher, as Dean Reynolds had. The only problem was *how* to do this.

Though Mother Meera had cracked me open and I'd had glimpses of another, vaster reality, I needed something else to get me through the night. Like Dean, I needed a regular practice that would calm my body, center my mind, and give me hope.

I tried everything.

Zen: During Sunday meditation sessions at the Zen Mountain Monastery in Mount Tremper, New York, I sat miserably staring at the wall while a bald nun walked around whacking people on the shoulder blades. Periodically, in an unbelievably shrill voice—like an insane dybbuk—she would shriek, *"Wake upppp!!!"* I counted my breaths and hated the rigidity, the dynastic name-dropping, the bowing and the scraping. When it was over, I watched the *roshi*, an ex-sailor covered with tattoos, zoom around the grounds on a golf cart, smoking Benson & Hedges.

Vipassana: I enrolled in a nine-day silent *vipassana*—or mindfulness—meditation retreat, at Southern Dharma, a rustic center in the Smoky Mountains of North Carolina, led by John, an American who'd been a Buddhist monk in Thailand. To say that I resisted this practice is an understatement. After two days, I was twitching and squirming on my pillow like someone with Saint Vitus's dance. Sitting perfectly still on a hard cushion in a cold room for fourteen hours a day might be the path to one's true nature, as John advised, but after several days of this, I wasn't sure I wanted to find mine.

On the last day, John asked what the word *discipline* meant to us. "Hitler," said a middle-aged man with a Brooklyn accent. "Attila the Hun," seconded a grandmother with white hair. So much for the enlightened mind, I thought.

Immortalism: I sat in a room while a preacher who called himself Reverend Matt jumped around the stage of the Radiant Light Ministry in San Francisco, wearing leather pants and a Hawaiian shirt, exhorting a crowd of New Age dykes and queers—who screamed out and cheered him on like a rock star—that if they just *breathed* enough, rebirthing themselves through all the negativity inside their bodies, they could live forever. "Death is just an old *idea*," Matt insisted. "It's all in your mind, people!" I left before the end of the lecture.

Yoga Retreats: Cabbage soup at six o'clock in the morning under the dining room photograph of a master yogi holding his own intestines in his hands. Though I knew that self-disembowelment was not the goal of this practice, I was intimidated nonetheless. The daily regime involved four hours of twisting, breathing, contorting myself into unnatural positions in a drafty room. Extreme hunger and stiffness, leading to stiffness and extreme hunger. Early escape while the teacher was sleeping.

Kundalini Initiation: For $125 each, twenty other people and I sat with a woman in Santa Fe, chanting Sanskrit and meditating, then receiving instruction on the two hours of daily practice required at home for the serpent energy to blast up our spines and open our crown chakras. When the ceremony was over, this gentle lady placed a red rose on top of my head, which I balanced as best I could, walking back to my seat in front of the other initiates. Ten days later I burned out.

Hermitage: For two summers, I lived alone in a ten-by-fifteen-foot cabin in the woods outside Woodstock, reading Thoreau and Annie Dillard, trying to commune with nature. I hoped that through sheer isolation, removed from city distractions, I would be forced to settle down and *see* in the Zen way—the trees, the woodchuck, the stream trickling in the distance. What I saw, in actuality, was that I was going berserk.

Twelve Steps: For several months, I attended meetings of Sex and Love Addicts Anonymous, where visitors introduced themselves with multihyphenated labels ("Hi, I'm Louise, a recovering daughter of an alcoholic-incest-survivor-romantic-compulsive-bulimic") and told long sad stories about their erotic mishaps, counting the days they had abstained. I was turned off by the recovery-speak and never got past the First Step.

These experiences left me frustrated. I longed for holy company, the direct hit of an enlightened master to recharge my batteries and restore my faith. Mother Meera was beginning to seem like a distant light.

I heard about another woman saint, Amritanandamayi Ma—or Ammachi (Little Mother)—who was scheduled to give *darshan* in New York. That evening, Carole and I arrived early at the Universalist Church on Central Park West and took our places on the floor along with several hundred other people. Men and women in saris and white dhotis prepared the stage for Ammachi's arrival; there were tamburas and a sitar to accompany the singing of devotional *bhajan* hymns, and a chubby Indian man with thick glasses overseeing the whole affair, checking mikes, smiling at the crowd as they assembled.

While we waited for Ammachi's entrance, I read up on who she was. Her story was archetypal—for a saint. Born into a poor village family forty years before, she'd had visions from an early age, repeating the names of Hindu deities until her family began to think she was mad. One night when Ammachi was ten, she went out walking on the beach near her village and, chanting the name of Krishna, fell senseless for an entire night. When she awake, she was quite a different girl, no longer the mooning acolyte, but an enlightened master. Since that time, she had been teaching at her ashram in Kerala—which had thousands of visitors every year—founding schools and charitable organizations, traveling around the world giving *darshan*.

I'd read this kind of thing before, of course—nearly every saint's life was marked by some kind of spontaneous initiation, such as Ammachi's, where the ripe soul seemed to drop in one clean gesture from the tree of ordinary consciousness into an ongoing state of bliss. Thereafter, if the awakening was real, their personal lives stopped and a selfless life of service began, characterized by superhuman endurance and unbounded energy. I read that Ammachi had been known to give *darshan* to thousands of people in one stretch, not moving from her chair for seventy-two hours straight, with no visible sign of fatigue.

Many miracles had been witnessed around her. One in particular struck me as wonderful: One day at her ashram, Ammachi was sitting on the ground with a circle of her close disciples when she caught sight of a man standing alone at the far end of the yard, watching her. The man was a leper in the later stages of his disease, covered with sores, too ashamed of his smell and appearance to come any closer.

Those present report that, upon seeing the man, Ammachi stood up and ran toward him with her arms outstretched. The man turned away. "No, Ma!" he called out, covering his rotting face. "Not too close. I'm unclean!" But Ammachi, ignoring his words, took the man against her breast and kissed his sores, holding him close for many minutes. She stroked his head and told him that he must visit her three times a week without fail. Every few days, the leper would appear as he'd been instructed, and Ammachi would keep him close by, touching him often, cooing like a protective mother. At the end of a month, observers reported ported that the leper's sores had closed and that his stumpy fingers were regenerating. At the end of six months, the man was completely cured, without so much as a scar on his body to show where the leprosy had been.

I closed the pamphlet and looked at the smiling photograph of Ammachi at the center of the stage. This was the power of holy love, I thought—not the love we talk about in romantic songs or even the love between close friends—but the love that can come only from a liberated being, a love without bounds or conditions, like the love I'd seen in Mother Meera's face, a love I had not, until that moment in Thalheim, believed was possible on this earth. That kind of love could indeed create miracles, healings of the body and mind and spirit. I turned from Ammachi's picture to Carole, who was lying on her back with her eyes closed—exhausted from the ten-block walk—her rosary in her hands folded across her chest. I thought of the Christian word for that kind of holy love—*agape*—and Ammachi putting her arms around my sick friend. For a second, I hoped.

A hush came over the hall as Ammachi entered from the back of the church. The crowd rose to its feet as the woman in the white sari bustled, smiling, toward the stage, touching bowed heads as she passed. She was small and chubby and very dark, barefoot, with a round childlike face, a large jewel in her left nostril, a white circle of powder across her forehead, and two strands of thick wooden beads around her wrists. She climbed the stairs to the stage and turned to face the crowd, flashed her wide smile, then gestured for everyone to be seated.

Her eyes closed, rocking from side to side with her face upturned, Ammachi began to sing, the group repeating with her. "*Jaya shiva om—ma ma—jaya shiva om—ma ma*," she sang, quietly at first, then more animatedly, until she seemed possessed by the music, drunk on the divine names she was singing. Now her hands were folded across her chest; now she was flinging them up toward the sky. Now her hands were folded under her cheek, shoulders raised, as if speaking to a lover on the pillow; now she was breaking the tune to whisper, "Shiva, Shiva, Shiva," into the microphone, or crying out for Krishna, then giggling to herself, as if the god had answered her.

Soon after the singing ended, *darshan* began. Unlike Mother Meera, whose style of touch was reserved, precise—almost scientific—Ammachi sat in a chair taking people into her arms and hugging them, rocking them, stroking their heads and whispering into their ears. Touched as I was by her holy appearance, I was, as always, on the lookout for any glitch in her behavior that might betray her. But she was exactly as one would imagine the mother of the world to be, opening her arms, taking each visitor to her breast, the milk of kindness flowing from her body. Carole and I watched her embrace Upper West Siders in yarmulkes, teenage girls with Walkmans, muscled gay men and toddlers, old people in wheelchairs, a girl who looked like Donna Summer in spandex knickers and a push-up bra.

When we reached the head of the line, Carole went first, shyly, laying her head on Ammachi's shoulder. I watched the small dark hands circle Carole's body, then pull her close and rock her back and forth, as if greeting a beloved child. When she finally let Carole go, I approached, feeling nervous.

The fear dissolved as soon as she grabbed me and nestled my head against her soft belly. I closed my eyes and smelled the faint sandalwood scent of her white cotton sari as she rocked me. My mind relaxed, and in that moment of surrender, a great feeling of relief passed through me. She lifted my head and brought it next to hers, then hissed into my ear, "Shiva, Shiva, Shiva," holding my face between her hands. Then she reached out and stuck a finger into a pot of sandalwood paste, pinned the gooey finger in the center of my forehead, and pushed my head straight back.

My mind went white. My eyes were open, looking into Ammachi's face as she stared at me with her brilliant smile, the light nearly outshining her face as she pushed my head farther and farther back until I thought I would faint. The room behind her head disappeared. I saw nothing but an enormous, fluorescent white moon with the outline of her face inside it. Then she let out a giggle, popped a Hershey's kiss into my mouth, and scattered a handful of flower petals over my head.

Ammachi's holy touch stayed with me. In the days after her *darshan*, I wandered around in a sort of afterglow, in which everyone on the street looked like a lover, a brother, a sister, a friend; the city itself seemed friendlier. I was unnaturally peaceful and at ease; my usual jittery pace slowed down to a stroll. Carole felt the same way—"like I'm carrying her inside of me," is how she put it. It was true; I felt as if the bliss streaming out of Ammachi's face had entered and uplifted me.

I began to notice something else, too. Ammachi's luminous presence made me remember the faculty that had been awakened in me in Thalheim and Mahabalipuram, which now, walking through the streets of New York, became obvious again. It was a kind of brightening, an illumination. As if my eyes had been pried open a couple of extra degrees, I began to glimpse patterns and synchronicities, an organizing principle at work, rendering the mundane surface of things completely magical—events, people, objects swirling and undoing themselves like flecks in a kaleidoscope before my eyes.

At times, I became inadvertently psychic—or simply hypersensitive—to the world around me. I would suddenly "know" things in unexpected flashes, or predict things without knowing how I was doing it. One day, I was walking down Fifth Avenue during rush hour, and the face of a man coming toward me seemed to stand out from the crowd, magnified, like a cutout pasted to a background where it didn't belong. The next night, a friend brought this man to dinner at my house. On the other occasions, I would think of someone whom I hadn't seen in months, walk out the door, and run straight into him. Once or twice, the thought occurred to me to call a particular person—I picked up the phone and found him on the other end, before the phone rang. In these uncanny moments, too frequent for my skeptical mind to deny, I was reminded that something had indeed changed in me; I did now perceive a design in the world I once believed chaotic, a force moving me and everything else in ways I could not control or understand. Reality suddenly seemed to cohere; it was the difference between seeing a piece of paper as a blank white collection of molecules or as an emanation of the cloud that rained to feed the tree from which it was harvested. This sacramental vision changed *everything*, breathing poetry back into the prosaic world, turning the flat material world into a hologram of wonder.

Still, there was the everyday business of coping with Carole's illness and my own declining T cells. When Carole got out of the hospital after two excruciating days on a gurney in the NYU emergency room (the hospital had no beds), passing a kidney stone caused by sulfa drugs, Robert suggested that we go with him to the Healing Circle, a group inspired by the work of Louise Hay that met every Wednesday night at a church in Chelsea. I was wary, but Robert convinced me that it was time for me to learn to "separate the message from the messenger."

Hay, a science-of-mind minister turned New Age Doris Day, had become rich and famous by telling people to heal their lives through self-love. While this message had its good points, however, the dark side of Hay's delivery was not unknown to me. Shortly before he died, John had come back from one of her weekend workshops in a deep depression.

"She told us that we were responsible for being sick," I remembered him saying. "She told us we had to find out why we wanted to get sick in the first place and that if we changed our thoughts, we could heal ourselves." John had gone to the workshop needing support and had come back with a guilty conscience. There was nothing new in the axiom that thoughts affect physical health, of course; what *was* offensive was the implication of blame that Hay's message may have carried, a kind of New Age feel-good, get-positive-and-live-forever fascism that caused many sincere but confused people to believe that healing was as easy as looking into a mirror—one of Hay's tricks— and affirming, "I love and respect myself exactly as I am."

Carole was feeling blue but willing to give it a try. She'd finally come to the conclusion that even if she was dying, she wasn't dead yet and would have to find some way of confronting her despair on a day-to-day basis.

"As long as they don't get all woo-woo," she said when I helped her from the cab on Eighteenth Street. "One word about pink lights and I'm out of there."

At the door of the church, a middle-aged man was handing people teddy bears. "Can I give you a hug?" he asked us.

Carole shot me a look that said, "I told you so," and let him embrace her. Then he wrapped his arms around me as if he'd known me since kindergarten and murmured *Mmmmmm*, into my ear.

"I'm so glad you came."

"Thanks," I said, pulling away.

"First time?" Carole and I both nodded. He handed us each a bear and a tiny hand mirror. "Just remember something. No matter what comes up for you in there, you are perfect exactly as you are."

"Oh, my God," whispered Carole, moving past him into the church.

Inside the darkened auditorium two hundred people were standing around, hugging, laughing. Gloria Gaynor's "I Will Survive" blared from the speakers, and here and there, someone was dancing disco style, twirling his arm like a rodeo rider with a lasso. In the center of the room, a man who looked Native American was constructing an altar of candles, feathers, stones, and religious paraphernalia, lighting sage and holding it up to the four directions. There were many faces that I knew from years past; only now the men I'd seen lounging in steam rooms or ordering beers at Uncle Charlie's were milling around with crystals hanging from their necks, hugging one another like nuns. How brilliant of gay men, I thought, to have found a new way to cruise in the midst of this virus. Now, "Got a light, buddy?" had been replaced as an opening line by "Have you *seen* the latest Shakti Gawain? Better than her last!"

We formed an enormous circle, joined hands, and were led in an affirmation prayer by an Israeli with a hypnotic voice, who guided us through inner space toward the golden light at the center of our foreheads. When we opened our eyes, everyone looked peaceful, and people started telling their stories. The theme was transformation: again and again, men and women, ranging from healthy to extremely ill, revealed how AIDS had activated positive changes in their lives, giving them "permission" to leave jobs, cities, and lovers; to discover in the quest for healing (if not a cure) who they were, what they wanted, and how they intended to spend the rest of their lives.

I was moved by these stories, proud of how our community had bonded together in crisis. But I detected something not quite honest in the tone of the meeting, a hint of false cheer, a reluctance to talk about the pain. Just as this thought crossed my mind, an emaciated man stood up and started screaming.

"I'm getting sick and tired of listening to this bullshit every week," he shouted, scaring the people around him.

"Do you have something to share?" asked the Israeli moderator.

"No, I don't have anything to *share*," said the man sarcastically. "I have something to say."

"Please say it then. Without judgment."

The sick man glared. "Have you ever been sick?" he asked the man with the mellifluous voice.

"No," he answered.

"Do you know what it's like to be in a hospital for six weeks with a hundred-and-four fever, puking all over yourself, with a catheter in your gut?"

The moderator shook his head.

"No, you don't. And yet you sit here talking to *me* about positive thinking and finding my spirit. When I'm depressed, you tell me it's just the dimming of light. When I'm in pain, you tell me it's there to teach me something. When I tell you I'm scared to die, you tell me it's just a passing thought. You've got a fucking platitude for every complaint in the book because you're afraid of what it feels like to just hurt, plain simple hurt—not noble, not righteous, just stinking pain."

The room fell silent. The man started to weep. "I came here to be with people like me, but now I find out you don't want to tell the truth either. There's no place for me now, 'cause I can't think positive. I'm scared. I'm not a hero. I'm just dying." The man broke down sobbing, and the woman next to him put her arms around his shoulder. I heard whimpering and saw that Carole was quietly crying, too. This guy was telling the truth, I realized. These well-meaning people were covering up plain old death, in an effort to cope, dressing it up in the banner of enlightenment, making it heroic, not allowing it simply to be what it is, without cosmetics.

More than ever, I realized that if dying was to become my teacher, I needed to look it straight in the face and see what was really there, beyond philosophy or positively serene.

EIGHTEEN

"**B**ERNADETTE DIGGINS?" I asked when I arrived for my first day of training as a volunteer at Cabrini Hospice. The chubby woman behind the desk pushed a pack of Kools under her pile of papers and smiled up at me.

I had talked over my confusion about death with Stephen Levine, who suggested that I spend some time on the front lines. The idea appealed to me immediately. Maybe some experience working with the dying—rather than just listening to people talk about it—would teach me what I needed to learn for Carole and myself.

Bernadette gave me a tour of the place, which consisted of one long hall with twenty-five rooms. On the walls were mementos of patients who had come and gone, and a big quilt that said LOVE UNTIL YOU DROP. All the beds were occupied by patients—black, white, old, young—whose eyes followed us as we strolled past. Some made movements with their hands as if to wave, some scowled, some were sleeping. On the rooms of the AIDS patients were signs that warned workers to take "enteric precautions."

"They come here at the end," said Bernadette back in her office. "Most of our patients die within two weeks of arrival. We give no extraordinary measures here and try to make the place as homey as possible." I had noticed plants, religious items, afghans, posters in the rooms to personalize them. I thought of what the word *hospice* means—a resting place along the way where the weary traveler is offered comfort.

The training took ten weeks. We were taught what to say and not to say to terminal patients, how to change diapers, how to lift a dying body into a wheelchair and speak to grieving families. Sister Marietta, a fat lady in black orthopedic shoes, told us about Cabrini's approach to spiritual counsel.

"We don't do anything to convert people here," she said. "You help patients with whatever faith they bring. I've had Buddhists and Muslims and atheists, not that I knew what to say to them, but you do the best you can. Most of the time I just hold their hands and let them talk—that's what they mostly want anyway. Comfort of another human being, just like you and me."

After the spirit was attended to, Mary, the head nurse, said, physical pain was the next most challenging issue. Mary was a no-nonsense lady with glasses hanging from a chain around her neck.

"Most of you have no idea whatsoever what chronic pain is like," she explained. "You get hurt, you wait, you get better. But imagine if you didn't get better. Imagine if you were *never* going to get better— the pain was worse than you could possibly imagine and nothing would take it away." She came over and, without warning, punched me in the arm with her knuckles. "You see how that feels?" she asked me. I nodded, rubbing the spot. "Imagine that pain all the time all over your body—you're in bed and it's only going to get worse. That is chronic pain, and that's what you're going to see in some of these patients, so prepare yourselves. And one last thing: whatever you do, never, ever tell a dying person that you know how they feel. You don't. You must respect that difference between you."

The hospice was strange but also familiar. The atmosphere—inert, crisis pending in the background—reminded me of the house where

I grew up, where everything, it had seemed, was always poised on the brink of death. I made friends with the Jamaican nurses, Big Betty and the Brick (because she was shaped like one), who flirted with me and caught me as I snooped around, reading people's files. Knowing all about the patients' insides before I'd even met them fascinated me. Knowing, for instance, the date when Sandra in 103B, whose daughter has signed the paper donating her organs (Xerox included in file), first found the tumor on her tongue, then tracing the spread of the disease from page to page, year to year, procedure to procedure, until now, when you knock and enter the room where a white-haired woman is turned on her side, staring at a television set, face taped from nostrils to chin. You know her insides, her history, her data, but you do not know her and never will, because the next day when you come on duty, her bed is empty, the sheets crisp, and there is an index card on the board with her name on it, giving the time of her death. Every day, there are new cards, and files to be put away.

Strange things happened. One day I was sitting in the room of a woman who was sleeping, reading a magazine, waiting for her to wake up. A young man walked in and said, "What are *you* doing in here?"

"Waiting for her to wake up," I said.

"She's dead!" her grandson said, staring at me like I was some kind of ghoul. "Get the hell out of here!"

I ran out and told Brick, who was unfazed (the woman had died an hour before). "Come help me, sonny," she said.

Brick and I returned to the room. In one swift movement, she pulled the lady's nightgown off, leaving her naked on the bed. As if she were trussing a chicken, Brick lifted the dead woman's feet up and swiped between her legs with a rag, humming while she did it.

"How many times have you done this?" I asked.

"Too many times, honey."

"No really, how many?" I asked, appalled as she let the legs down and folded the woman's hands across her chest. "A hundred? A thousand?"

"Let me see," Brick said, putting her hand on her hip. "I been doing this twenty-two years. We get about seventy dead a month. You figure it out. Uh oh!" Just then, the room was filled with a terrible stench, and I saw an ooze of brown fluid come out of the dead woman's rump. "Get me a chuck, quick."

I ran out of the room and down the hall. I riffled through cupboards and closets without success. Finally, Big Betty handed me a blue absorbent pad.

"Oh, honey, she a geyser," said the Brick as she soaked up the mess. When the old woman's body was washed, another nurse, Pepita, came in with a black bag. I watched the two nurses slip the bag under the corpse's legs, up and over her shoulders. When the zipper was secure, they tied a piece of twine around the ankles and waist. Then Brick asked me to do the honors, dangling a third piece of rope over the woman's throat.

"No, thanks," I said.

"Please, honey." They both stood there looking at me expectantly. "We superstitious. It like a hangman. I don't know why, but it give me the creeps."

I took the string from her hands, tied it around the dead woman's neck.

"Not too tight, honey," said the Brick. I loosened the string. A few minutes later, the morgue guys came with a gurney and took the woman away.

*

The time at the hospice was mostly quiet, long and uneventful—like dying itself. I made friends with a gay priest named Horacio, who was at the end of a ten-year struggle with AIDS. Little more than a skeleton, he lay now, day after day, staring at the second hand turning on the face of the clock. I couldn't help but see myself in him; a religious man, a gay man, reduced to this: a body on a bed, watching time pass until he dies.

One day, Horacio asked if I was afraid to die. I was apprehensive about admitting this to a dying man at first, but I sensed that his priest self could see through me, and that there was no use lying.

"Yes, I am" I said, rubbing his swollen, purple feet with lotion.

"Don't be," said Horacio.

That was all he said, but during the weeks I sat with Horacio, I began to repeat those words to myself like a mantra with multiple meanings: don't be, don't be, don't be. I watched Horacio's gentle face, his humor and wisdom in the midst of physical wasting, and sensed that here, in this priest's eyes, was a hint of what I was looking for—strength and calm in the face of death—and something else as well. The last time I saw Horacio, I brought him a single red rose for the vase sitting empty at his bedside. I shall never forget the look on his face when he saw it, as if I had walked in with a Rembrandt.

"*O Dio,*" he said to me, smiling as I filled the vase, put the flower in, and pushed it close enough for him to see from his pillow without having to turn his head. His eyes were huge and luminous as they gazed at the petals, and I perceived, quite distinctly, that Horacio was not this dying body; that, in fact, the ravaging of his body had only served to thin the veil between his spirit and the world. With less bone and muscle to veil it, the light in his eyes showed through more brightly; watching Horacio watch the flower, I could actually see the love pouring out of him, this spirit in him that was not the flesh. This discrepancy between the dying body and the light within it shocked me, revealing, without a word, what I already suspected: that this rapture in Horacio's spirit could not be killed, that the thing that saw from inside this skull was perfectly indestructible—the *atman* itself.

Without a word, watching Horacio, I was given the answer to a question that had haunted me since I was five years old. Lifting the lid of a garbage can and seeing my first dead thing—a blue jay wrapped in newspaper—I'd stood there a long time, staring at its cat-chewed body, wondering where the *thing* had gone that made it fly. I remember wondering whether the bird was this pile of bloody feathers or the thing that had escaped. Now, I knew.

Working with the dying and dead brought up the question of reincarnation. Did I believe that I would be reborn, and was there any comfort in this? Not especially. It was not as if a belief in reincarnation made living or dying any easier, since it wasn't the personal ego that survived in any case (as if *that* would be a comfort). Still, I couldn't help but wonder.

My deepest intuition was that something certainly persisted, but it wasn't myself. This life-form had no identity but was rather a kind of morph, a cluster of memory: energy that would continue traveling after my heart had stopped beating. I did not see the "soul's journey" as a literal phenomenon, in which the soul is schooled from one body to the next until, *poof,* it graduates one day to godhood. To my mind, such concepts were mere words to describe an uncontainable and nameless process of light and sound in everlasting motion.

It was my belief that man contained within himself the building blocks of life below him, the attributes of all other creatures. We were, in fact, the sum of creation; just as the flower rises from the plant but also transcends it, so every human being had coded within himself the entire evolutionary plan: the flight of the eagle, the diligence of the ant, the fierceness of the mantis, the lethargy of the sloth, the night vision of the cat, the viciousness of the piranha, the music of the nightingale, the latency of the caterpillar, the self-destructiveness of the lemming, the moon hunger of the wolf, the vanity of the peacock.

In this way, it seemed to me that each one of us was a reincarnation of not only this specific cluster of experience—a microcosm of particulars—but of the macrocosm as well, a reincarnation of every creature that had passed before us. Thus, we were reincarnated in more than one sense, mulched from the dead, our lives rising from their memory. I was a reincarnation of my parents, grandparents and distant ancestors, the continuation of a song that did not begin with me and would not die with me, but continued in everything I touched.

I went to see Dr. Weissman on February 10, 1988, for my blood-test results and was told that my T cells were half of what they'd been the year before, still in the normal range, but just barely. He asked me if I would consider going on AZT if they dropped any further. Carole had been taking this drug for a couple of months, and even though it had given her kidney stones, it had also restored her energy; on a recent afternoon, she'd actually golfed nine holes and told me afterward that, standing on the course with a putter in her hand, looking over the perfectly groomed lawns warmed by sunlight, she felt almost as if she'd been reborn. "I never saw anything so beautiful in my life," she told me. I told Dr. Weissman that I'd cross the AZT bridge when I came to it.

*

In April, Carole called me with the scariest news yet.

"I've got something to tell you," she said.

She had The Tone. "Tell me."

Carole paused, and I got that sick feeling when hot phlegm rises in your throat. "What is it?"

"Lesions," she said.

"What do you mean, lesions?"

She breathed deeply, "The doctor says I have lesions growing in my brain. Toxoplasmosis."

This explained a lot. In spite of her renewed energy, over the past few months Carole had been forgetting things and feeling disoriented. At first when she told me she felt dizzy, I laughed and asked her how she could tell the difference. She'd always been chronically scattered in a charming way, like Diane Keaton in *Annie Hall*. But lately, this charm had turned to real confusion. She'd get out of cabs, drop her keys in the street, and start sobbing uncontrollably. Other times, she'd trail off in midsentence, confusing memories. I tried to chalk it up to the battery of medications she was taking, but in my heart I feared that something was more seriously wrong, that some form of dementia was taking Carole away.

In order to determine how bad the toxo was, Carole needed a spinal tap. The doctor doing the procedure was Indian, which made us both feel oddly safer, as if he'd be muttering mantras while he inserted the needle. Carole curled into the fetal position on the examining room table and asked if I could stay. The doctor agreed and I pulled a chair alongside, as I'd done a dozen times before. He touched her back with a swab of Mercurochrome and she jumped at the cold, then relaxed as he painted the blood-colored liquid in a swath across her back.

"I've always wanted to go to India," Carole said.

"Beautiful country," he said, picking up a needle that made my stomach drop.

"Mark has been."

"Yes?" he said, tipping his head from side to side. "Vacation?" I nodded and stroked Carole's arm as he studied her spine. "This will hurt," he said.

"Thanks for telling me."

"But only for a second."

"That's what my husband said."

"Hold her," he said to me. Carole gripped my hand. The doctor poised the tip of the three-inch needle at the bottom of Carole's coccyx, nodded at me, and pushed the thing in to the hilt. Carole whimpered, her body tightened. The pain went through me.

"Relax, ma'am. Please."

Her eyes bulged. I watched the clear fluid fill the syringe.

Afterward, to distract herself for the requisite hour, Carole talked to me obsessively about what color she should paint her kitchen. "Ivory or peach?" she offered, not waiting for an answer. "I've never really thought of myself as a peach person. Do you think of me as a peach person?"

I'd learned to humor Carole in these times, but her evasions left me frustrated. I wanted to know more about how it felt to be inside her body, what she was coming to understand, what haunted her in the middle of the night—more for my sake than for hers. Since it was Carole who was leading me into this new territory, I hungered for more detailed reports, a topographical map of what she was discovering there.

But as I was learning, the big questions are the last thing most sick people want to talk about. Dying people don't sit around talking about dying. They talk about Sally Jessy Raphael; they talk about shopping; they talk about the weather, or their cat: anything *but* their own demise. They know they're dying, but they're still living, too, and philosophizing about mortality is an emotional luxury they can't always afford. Rapidly though she was declining, Carole was nonetheless more concerned with how her hair looked, or what movie to see at the Ten-Plex, than with the existential implications of what was happening.

NINETEEN

I N T H E W I N T E R of 1991, Carole seemed to be stable, and I felt the need to return to India. For the past four years, my life in New York had been an almost nonstop series of shocks and dislocations that left me scrambling to maintain the mystic view. Diligently as I tried to strengthen this connection, my environment overwhelmed me often, making India, Mother Meera, even Alexander seem like entities from another life. I desperately needed to remind myself that they weren't.

I was broke, however, and would need a minor miracle to get there. As it happened, I heard a rumor that the Indian government sent journalists on all-expenses-paid junkets in order to promote tourism. After weeks of bureaucratic finagling, I received a voucher in the mail for a ticket to Bombay.

My ulterior motive for this voyage was to visit Benares, where Alexander and I had meant to go before our falling-out. Known to the ancients as Kashi (City of Light), Benares is the oldest inhabited city on earth and considered to be among the holiest as well. In particular, Benares is famous as a pilgrimage site for the dying. For nearly ten thousand years, Hindus have gone there to live and wait out their last days, and afterward to be cremated along the banks of the River Ganges. It is said that to die in Benares promises a happy rebirth, and some thirty-five thousand bodies are disposed of every year at the two crematoria along the river. To make my own pilgrim-age to Benares now seemed urgent. I sensed that there was something I needed to learn there, watching the corpses go up in flame—some teaching that might help me cope with what lay ahead.

I landed in Bombay and was greeted again by that unmistakable flower-and-bones smell that had struck me on my arrival in India five years before. After taking a flight to Benares, I made my way to the Harishchandra ghat, where the cremations were performed, and was wandering in a narrow street when a man in a Michael Jackson T-shirt pulled me aside.

"Lodging, sir?"

His name was Bhose, and he ran a squalid little pension, the Yogi Lodge, just a few steps away. In its tiny, smoky office, he took my pass-port, and when he saw from my visa that I was a writer, the floodgates opened.

"I know what you want in Benares," Bhose said. "You want to find God. Everyone comes here to find God, but God's not here, God's not anywhere. I don't believe in God. I've met so many great people. I've met Mother Teresa, Anandamayi Ma, the Daily Dilemma."

"Who?"

"The Dalai Lama. I've met all these people, but they don't do nothing for me." This obnoxious little man lit a cigarette and offered me a beer, though it was only 7 A.M. "This is nineteen ninety-one, man, wake up and smell the coffee. I mean, Benares is shit."

"I thought it was supposed to be holy," I said.

"That's just tourist stuff. There's no such thing as holy. Not India, not now. They're all a bunch of crooks."

Bhose depressed me, and I left him as soon as I could dump my backpack, and wound my way down past the *chi* stalls, cattle, dogs, and beggars clogging the street. A bus careened by me streaming cellophane flags, garish cartoon versions of the goddess Durga riding her tiger painted on the front. Children ran after the sacred cows, scooped up their turds, and carried them to the gutter, where they squatted, laughing and patting the dung into burger-shaped lumps to sell as fuel for fires. The place looked surreal through my jet-lagged haze—even more so when I reached the river.

A man stood half naked in the brown Ganges, brushing his teeth and spitting, while the bloated corpse of a cow floated by belly up. A group of old women in white—who I assumed had come from the widows' ashram up the hill—walked by me on the way to their morning ablutions. Holy men in *lungi* skirts stood waist deep, dipping themselves, chanting prayers, cupping the water in their hands, and holding it up in offering, while a boat of Japanese tourists slid by, cameras poised and clicking. Everywhere were the *doms*, the caste below the untouchables, who preside over the cremation grounds. Groups of *doms* were asleep under their carts, while their children surrounded me in swarms, filthy, with strangely ancient faces, holding out their hands for rupees. A little girl sat in the dust next to a scrawny dog turned on her side, covered with a litter of puppies, next to a smoking pit. A group of teenage boys were playing stickball with bones—human or other, I couldn't tell.

A short distance down the river, I saw a family sitting on the ground by a corpse bound in white and strapped to a bamboo litter, and headed toward them for a closer look. When I ventured too close, however, a member of the family—a handsome young man in a spotless white outfit—shooed me away. I took a seat at a polite distance from the proceedings and observed.

Once the body had been immersed for a last time in the river, a Brahmin priest anointed it and prayed; when he gave the signal, the corpse was hoisted onto the pyre and covered with saffron and flowers. The young man in white (whom I took to be the eldest son) circled the body, then took a lit stick from a priest and touched it to the woodpile. I watched as the kindling slowly began to catch fire, then the logs, and finally the fabric enshrouding the corpse, which fell away gradually to reveal the body underneath: its charred face, the nose hooked and narrow like a mummy's. The deceased was a woman, I saw now, watching with fascination as this extraordinary process took place in full public view, without sentimentality or wailing (considered bad luck for the dead). I watched for a long time as the flames rose to consume this woman and her family watched her disappear. When finally nothing was left but bones and cinder, the young man threw a clay pot of water over his shoulder onto the smoldering pyre and walked away from the cremation site, followed by the rest of the family. No one looked back.

I sat there mesmerized by what I'd just seen, wondering whether I could ever be this matter-of-fact about the death of someone I loved. Staring at the river, I remembered a story about a saint named Ramakrishna who lived close to this spot at the turn of the century. Sitting by the Ganges one day, gazing at the river as I was doing now, Ramakrishna had seen a beautiful woman emerge from the water and come toward him, radiant and naked. As she approached, her body swelled to the point of bursting, and a child appeared between her legs. As Ramakrishna looked on, the woman of the river took the infant up to her breast and suckled it; then, just as simply, she broke the child's neck with her bare hands and, transformed into Kali—the dark mother—she consumed the child before his eyes. When the infant's blood and bones were gone, the goddess turned and walked back into the river.

I was strangely comforted by this story and by the raw extremity of what I'd just seen in real life. There was relief in the naked truth—shock, but revelation, too, in the fact of it. Mortality was just a word, but this heap of smoking dust was more. If I could accept *this*, I thought, turning from the cremation site back toward the Yogi Lodge—if I could pass through the incomprehensibility of this process and stand on the other side—nothing could scare me anymore. I would be free.

When I returned, Bhose interrogated me as to where I'd been. "To the barbecue?" he asked with a cynical wink.

Three days later, having watched half a dozen more cremations, I left Benares for the south, in no way suspecting how much further this initiation had to go.

I flew to Bhubaneswar in the state of Orissa and boarded the Coromandel express to Madras. It promised to be the sort of twenty-hour Indian train ride I loved: a sleepless day and night on a bare wood seat, the train chugging through village after village, with unexplained two-hour stops, testing your limits and dropping you into a twilight zone of tedium, endurance, and surrender. I settled in for the duration with a pack of Gold Flake cigarettes and a novel.

In Madras, I caught the bus to Mahabalipuram. I hoped to recapture the peace and joy I had felt there with Alexander, to pay a kind of homage to our weeks there, for old time's sake. Unfortunately, this was not to be. What I found, once I had installed myself in a bungalow at the Ashok Palace and set out along the sand toward town, was nothing like the Mahabalipuram I remembered. Little had changed outwardly: the woman selling stuffed rats on the main road was still there; the busloads of Indian pilgrims were still arriving hourly and pouring into the Shiva Temple; nubile, bare-chested boys still pedaled their rickshaws up and down the main street, naked under their cotton skirts; and everywhere, still, was the sound of the stonesmiths' chiseling hammers, etching out images of the gods in stone. Yet, this place had changed. For me, without Alexander and his ecstatic personality, Mahabalipuram seemed flat and empty, a pale outline of the paradise I remembered.

I went to the hotel where Alexander and I had stayed. Our room had been hit by a hurricane: the roof was down, the glass of the patio door broken. The place where we sat naked, writing and listening to music, was filled with shredded clapboard and glass. I went to the spot behind the sculpture caves where Alexander and I had often watched the sun set over the rice paddies, but found only Germans in Birkenstocks, slugging beers and shouting at the top of their lungs.

Reconciling myself to the fact that my idyll in Mahabalipuram was going to be a disappointment, I returned to my room hoping to rest, but was plunged, instead, into one of the most terrifying experiences of my life.

Feeling lonesome and anonymous on the other side of the globe, I did what I had done as a child when I needed company: I went to the mirror to talk to myself. Sitting down in front of the glass, I was panicked instead by what I saw: with my face half in shadow, I looked twenty years older than I was; haggard, sunken-eyed, cheekbones drawn and hollow. In that moment my face looked irreversibly damaged, unmistakably terminal. I saw death in my face then, like a darkness that had settled over my features. Hard as I tried to stare it down, write it off as fatigue, imagination, terrible lighting, I couldn't. Death was there inside my skin.

Suddenly I was overwhelmed by animal fear, wondering if I had crossed the terminal line without knowing it. Was the virus visible in me? Could other people see? Passing me, did they think to themselves, that man is dying, as I did twenty times a day in Manhattan?

Was I kidding myself into thinking otherwise? From the bony face staring back at me from the mirror at this moment, I thought not.

Then it got worse. As I stared at my reflection, not moving a muscle, the image in the glass began to flatten out, as if it were a photograph, a picture in a newspaper obituary, tucked away in a box. As I watched, the photograph began to yellow, crack, and curl up around the edges. Frozen there, I saw that this outline really was *me*; this fading image was my body. Thinking this, I heard a phrase in my mind, "All of this will soon be gone," and with these words came another vision.

I closed my eyes and saw below me thousands upon thousands of naked people crammed together, extending as far as the eye could see. Their gaunt faces were turned up toward the sky as they swayed to a kind of celestial music, waves of angelic voices rising and falling in exquisite harmony. "All of this will soon be gone," the voice repeated. "This is the final truth, a last communion of skin and bones." Watching this mass of humanity stripped down to its barest essence, bodies nearly identical before death, I saw that, stripped of illusion, this was the sum of the human condition—that I was part of that great mortal swarm, swaying naked to that same music. The inescapable truth of this seemed to enter my body, flattening me, making me feel physically ill.

Then the experience changed again, and where there had been this mass of naked humanity, there was a sort of blank screen, with a flat white line extending across it. At the right side of this frame, the white line jolted up a bit, then disappeared off the screen. I "knew" somehow that this blip signified the moment of death—and that the rest of this line, till the very last moment, represented life. Contemplating this picture, I realized how completely absurd it was to walk along that line anticipating nothing but the blip! The blip was nothing but a parenthesis, not even an end to the sentence. With this insight came a flood of enormous relief. Much of my fear had arisen from obsession with the blip, I saw then, anticipating it, giving it power over my mind.

Afterward, I wrote in my journal: "When he saw that in this great panorama of life, he had been doing nothing but fearing a point the size of a pin, he had a good Buddhist laugh and died."

In Bangalore, I was relieved to have my solitude broken. My plane was met, like a VIP's, by a car, driver, and government guide.

"We are happy to see you, Mr. Mark," said the guide, Dr. Pushpa, a young woman with pockmarked skin and enormous sunglasses. "We have been here since yesterday, waiting."

"You don't know how happy I am to see *you*," I said, squeezing her hand.

"But your itinerary had you in Bangalore yesterday."

What could I say? That I'd been locked in a bungalow on the beach hallucinating my own death? "Mahabalipuram is a strange place," was all I could offer by way of explanation. "I just couldn't get away."

"I'm not surprised," Pushpa replied, shooing a group of beggar children away from my feet as we crossed the street to her old Ambassador. "You know, of course, that Mahabalipuram is sacred to Shiva, the Destroyer."

I nodded.

Pushpa was eyeing me closely from behind her glasses to figure out, I suspect, what kind of character she was dealing with. "You are interested in philosophy, Mr. Mark?"

"It's the only thing I'm interested in."

"Marvelous," she said. "Then we will very much enjoy ourselves. I am a doctor of philosophy."

"Really?" Pushpa couldn't have been thirty.

"And of law," she said.

"Why are you doing this then?"

"My father is old; there is little work. It is only temporary."

That night I slept well for the first time in weeks, and met Pushpa refreshed, early the next morning, in the hotel lobby. We set out from Bangalore toward Mysore, and en route, chugging past jungle and fields, honking and veering around bullock carts and beggars, we began to discuss Hinduism.

"I just don't get all the gods," I said. "The mythology doesn't interest me."

"That's a pity," Pushpa said. "As you must know, these gods are metaphors of mind, nothing more. The Hindu system is more complex and sophisticated than most people suspect. It functions on many levels. For the common man in his hut," she said, looking out the window at a passing village, "with his family deity, the image itself—Ganesha, Krishna, Shiva, Hanuman—is real. There is a direct connection between that image and his worship, a focus for his devotion. But these are simple people, and for the simple of heart, that is enough. As people become more sophisticated, however, these gods reveal themselves as symbols, gestures of consciousness, if you will, various aspects of the human psyche."

Later, at the Lalitha Mahal palace, covered ground to pinnacle with extraordinary carved images, Pushpa showed me what she meant. We stopped in front of a painting of a female god with dozens of hands, each one holding a different instrument. "This is mother Kali," she said.

"I recognize her," I replied, focusing on Kali's black face, fangs jutting out from her open mouth, remembering the dream I'd first had of Mother Meera ripping me apart like a doll.

"Just as Kali has a thousand hands, so can this painting be viewed in a thousand ways—like a Chinese box that keeps revealing smaller forms and contents." Pushpa continued. "To one man, she is a goddess; to another, the Jungian or the Buddhist, for example, she is a mandala of mind, a kind of blueprint of consciousness. This hand is holding a sword. It is the sword that Kali uses to slay the ignorant mind and birth the enlightened consciousness."

"I see."

"It is not important to believe literally in the Hindu pantheon. Once you penetrate the form and enter the meaning, it is fathomless; it predates Freud and the Western approach to psychology by millennia. But so many Westerners are fooled. They think of us as strange people with dots on our foreheads, caste systems, and interminable names. They see only the folk dimension of the faith, which is as misguided as believing that all devotees of Christ have artificial mangers in their living rooms. Unfortunately, as you see by all the ghastly pop art around, Hinduism lends itself particularly well to kitsch. But what doesn't, in the end, Mr. Mark? Now I'll leave you a moment to contemplate what I've said."

Pushpa turned and left me in the near dark of the inner temple, in front of the painting of Kali. Gazing up at the thousand-year-old image, I saw exactly what she meant. It was suddenly obvious that this figure had little or nothing to do with the kind of idolatry I'd attributed to the Hindu faith. Viewed as Pushpa instructed, these images appeared as reflections of a hidden light, flickerings on the screen of maya, like the shadows of Plato's cave, hinting at the ideal behind them. I thought of the photograph of Anandamayi Ma holding a figure of the goddess Durga to her heart, a piercing rapture on her wrinkled face, and of the photograph's caption that read: "Worship is not a ritual; it is an attitude, an experience."

This wasn't superstition but an archetypal process, the means by which mankind identifies with the divine, the alchemy turning the stone of ordinary things to gold. It was happening, I realized, at every level, at every moment. Viewed with the mystic eye, the tawdry, mortal realm might become a paradise indeed, a cartoon elephant, a god.

Pushpa was impressed when I told her all this in the car on the way to Mysore. "There are infinite ways to truth," she said. "Your turn of mind is toward *advaita*, nonduality, the path of *jnana*. There are many paths—*bhakti*, devotion; *karma*, service—appropriate for different temperaments. The *jnani* wishes for the direct path; he is attracted to formlessness and inquiry."

"Like Ramana Maharshi."

"Yes, like that great man. But remember that the Maharshi saw the mountain where he lived as Shiva. To attain *jnana*, the seeker must not exclude the other paths."

"That's exactly what I've been trying to do."

"Then you must understand both the relative and the absolute, without excluding either. In his quest for the absolute, the arrogant man tends to wipe everything clean, destroying the details in the name of the One. This is, unfortunately, the male way," said Pushpa, echoing Alexander's ongoing theme. "To disregard the things of the earth, the physical details bound up with death and pain and connection, in order to transcend. This is what many yogis do—those who are unbalanced. You have been to Benares?"

"Yes. It's a filthy mess."

"Precisely. The Mother, the Ganga, is left fetid and polluted, while the yogis prattle on about divinity. Hinduism does not promote this. It instructs us to serve the Mother in all her aspects as well as the

Father, understanding these to be symbols of the godhead. Look at the Hindu trinity: Shiva, Brahma, Vishnu; Destroyer, Creator, Preserver; head, heart, wisdom. Neither the head nor the heart are enough; wisdom is the balance of both. In Hinduism, for example, we understand that sometimes it is wise to lie, to cheat, to steal, even to kill. Wisdom transcends the ideas of right and wrong; it is always paradoxical."

"What isn't?" I asked.

"God is not. God is beyond paradox. He is nameless, formless, beyond opposites. Both this and that and neither. But I must be tiring you?"

"Not at all. I'm starved for this. Most of the time I feel like I'm out of my element. Half of me is running around in my life, while the other half is obsessed with these questions. It's a constant battle."

"It needn't be."

"It isn't for you?"

"When it was new, yes. When I began, I was passionate for God. I went to the Himalayas and climbed mountains. I lived for twenty days on chapati and pickle. But when I got to the top, I saw something."

"What?"

"I saw that it was not I who had conquered the mountain, but the mountain that had conquered me. It is not we who do this, Mr. Mark. It is He who does it through us. We are, in effect, God conquering Himself, and once you realize this, you begin to relax. There need be no conflict between religious and worldly life, since both are real."

"That's easy to say, but the fact is that the values of one do not necessarily work in the other. Religion says be selfless and detached; the world says achieve and compete. I feel like I'm walking a tightrope between opposite worlds."

"But both worlds are *true*," Pushpa insisted. "It is simply a matter of perspective. There's nothing noble in poverty; but until a man knows that it is not he, but He, who operates through him, his misunderstanding will bring him suffering and all the fruits of his labor will sour. The man who knows God, however, may prosper or not prosper without adding an ounce to the suffering of the world.

"Please, Mr. Mark, think about it. Imagine a smith making an infinite number of shapes from a quarry of gold—humans, cars, trees, and birds—then imagine the human form believing that he is other than gold himself. There you have the delusion of human beings." Pushpa glanced sideways to see if I was following her train of thought. "You're frowning, Mr. Mark."

I was torn, impressed by Pushpa's wisdom, but conflicted too. What she was saying was easy enough to accept in a country where the sacred was ordinary and the Other had a place setting at every table, but what about in the world where I lived, where progress on the spiritual track was barely recognized, let alone rewarded? Since my return to New York, it had been a constant struggle to maintain a faith, to cleave to the holy.

I tried to explain this to Dr. Pushpa as we walked around the grounds of Mysore palace, its outline illumined by a hundred thousand lights, a skeleton of grandeur against the balmy Karnataka sky, the air heavy with jasmine. To my surprise, she understood perfectly and insisted that my dilemma was common.

"Once again you are fooled by surfaces, Mr. Mark," she said. "India looks and smells holy. Certainly we have a tradition of holiness. But beneath the skin, she is as putrid as any beggar on the streets of New York. You're vain to believe that your struggle is more difficult than ours. You must stop being sentimental about your seeking. That's just another of the ego's tricks—to turn yourself into a martyr.

What you're describing is simply the human condition, nothing more, nothing less." Pushpa turned to scrutinize me. "You have met a teacher, am I correct?"

"How did you know?"

"I can see it in your eyes. The snake has bitten you. You are being drawn forward along a path you do not understand and against which you rebel. But since that meeting you have been unable to think of anything else with real love, is that right?"

"Yes," I said, surprised that Pushpa knew all this.

"And what is drawing you forward, Mr. Mark?"

"I have no choice," I said. "I mean, I have no time. I may be ill."

Pushpa didn't flinch. "Yes," she said. "I see."

"I've met a master—at least I *think* she's a master—but I'm confused."

"Why?" asked Pushpa, inviting me to join her on a bench outside the palace gates.

"Because I don't know if she's *my* master, Dr. Pushpa. I don't even know if I need a master."

"Ah, this is an important question. There are many schools of thought on this issue. Not everyone needs a guru, it is true, but for most of us, a teacher is helpful. Particularly at the beginning."

"What confuses me is that this woman doesn't really teach," I said, "at least not in the conventional sense." I explained how Mother Meera gave *darshan* in silence, how she encouraged her followers to trust their own hearts, discouraging them from becoming too attached to her presence, pushing them to lead ordinary lives in the world.

"She sounds marvelous," Pushpa said.

"She *is* marvelous. But I need some answers, too, some guidance. I want her to confirm that I'm progressing."

"Then you must go to her, Mr. Mark, and ask your questions. If she's a genuine master, you will be given the guidance you need. But remember one thing."

"What's that?"

"You may be surprised by what she tells you. It may be in the form of a riddle."

"The last thing I need is another riddle in my life."

"But *this* riddle, if you answer it, will bring you joy," said Pushpa.

She smiled and looked away from where we were sitting, to the outline of the mountains against the deep indigo sky. The next morning, at the Bangalore airport, my guide walked me out to the tarmac and took my hand. "Do not worry, Mr. Mark," said Dr. Pushpa, peering at me from behind her sunglasses. "You will find what you are looking for."

"That would be wonderful," I said.

Then she turned quickly and walked away, disappearing from my life as unexpectedly as she'd entered it.

TWENTY

WHILE I WAS away, Carole had decided that it was time to leave New York. She could barely make it up the stairs to her apartment now; what's more, the lesions on her brain were spreading, taking away a little more of her eyesight each day. She decided to move to Seattle to be near her sister. I promised to visit as soon as I could.

"I'm all right," Carole promised me on the phone a few weeks later. "Really. I have Elsie." Elsie was the nurse who came in eight hours a day, cooked for her, and gave her the medication.

"What about the other sixteen hours?" I asked. It was hard for me now having her gone, not being able to help her myself.

"They pass. Slowly sometimes, but they pass."

"Carole?"

"Okay, it's tough." Her voice trailed off.

"Can't the girls come?"

"They've got their lives. Marcy will be here for Thanksgiving."

It was only August. It seemed unlikely, though one could never predict, that Carole would even be here in November, let alone in any condition to eat a turkey. "I want another Thanksgiving," she said.

"I know you do."

"You think I'll get it?"

"God willing."

I hung up feeling desolate, torn between my need to settle back into my own life and the knowledge that I should be by Carole's side. I wrestled with the pros and cons of going to Seattle; the next afternoon, when I could no longer avoid the truth, I reached for the phone to call Carole and tell her I'd come live with her. As I touched the receiver, the phone rang.

"Can you come?" she asked. "Soon?"

Before I left, I received another call, from someone I'd never met—a friend of a friend who was passing through town and wondered if we could get together for coffee. He was a writer, I assumed, and though I was in no position to give advice—being lost, broke, and unemployed—I agreed to meet him the following day.

"Adam Jensen," he said, walking straight up to my table. He was wearing shredded jeans and a homeboy cap pulled backward off his cute, unshaven, bar-mitzvah-boy face. He sat across from me, put his foot up on the table, and pulled out a pack of Camel Lights. "Mind if I smoke?"

"Not if you give me one."

He put two cigarettes in his mouth and lit them. We talked about his book idea and then, without warning, he said, "I want you to know you're extremely healthy."

"What are you talking about?"

"Extremely healthy," Adam repeated, nodding to himself, his eyes traveling up my forehead then around my skull, studying something. "Yeah, dude, you're gonna live a long time."

I was taken aback. "What are you talking about?"

"Wait. Didn't Alina tell you?"

"Tell me what?"

"Why I called. I mean, the dreams or anything?"

"What dreams?"

Adam kicked back his chair and laughed. "Whoa, is she a space case! What did you think we were doing here?"

"Having coffee."

"I had a dream that you were in, but you were my grandfather. I'm not sure what it meant, but I got your name and told Alina that I was supposed to meet this guy Mark. When I described you, she gave me your number."

"You're not serious."

"She should have warned you. I see stuff."

"What kind of stuff?"

"Thoughts. Information. It happens all the time, but I usually keep it to myself. This time, I knew I had to talk to you."

"About this dream?"

"Partly. I needed to clear something up for myself, but I did that already, when I saw you. But there's something else." He spoke off-handedly, making no effort to convince me of what he was saying. "You need to know that you're not in danger."

"Oh, really?"

"The disease isn't strong." Adam looked me straight in the eyes. "A friend of yours is very sick, though. You're going to take care of her."

I nodded.

"She's an older woman with freckles and she loves you very much."

"How do you know that?"

"It's obvious. Anyway, she loves you so much that she took the arrow for you."

"What arrow?"

"Do you believe in other lives?"

"Not literally."

"Well, wake up. You and this lady go way back. Last time you were together, there was some kind of fight. You were her wife, I think. You ran to help her and got hit by an arrow. She lived but you died. Now she's returning the favor."

"That's ridiculous," I said, but even as the words came out of my mouth, my stomach tightened, remembering something Carole had said to me once. Even though she knew it sounded crazy, she couldn't shake the idea that somehow she had gotten sick so that I wouldn't have to. The irony of our situations, the uncanny way that her disease had unfolded, with me there at every turn to nurse her, was strange enough; greater still was the sense we shared from the moment we met that we were joined in ways that were impossible to explain. We did not, in any obvious way, *belong* in each other's lives, yet we were inextricably bound by a sense of destiny that was sometimes eerie.

"Did Alina tell you about Carole?" I asked.

"Nope," said Adam, holding up his hand. "Scout's honor."

"Did she tell you I was HIV-positive?"

"No. But she did tell me that you were interested in spiritual stuff. Except, I gotta tell you, man, you've got a really thick skull. You think too friggin' much."

Just then, Adam looked at his watch and jumped up. "I've got a plane, man, too bad. I woulda liked to hang out. Good luck with your friend."

Carole looked tiny in her nightgown. She walked slowly now, teetering and holding the wall to keep from bumping into things. She felt her way from the bed to the sofa and settled down with a sigh.

"No energy," she said, catching her breath. She extended her leg to show me how thin the calf was, shrunk to a third its normal size. "Pathetic, huh?" she said, as if marveling at something not herself. "And my heinie? Forget about it."

"You don't look that bad," I said honestly. The truth was that although Carole had wasted a great deal, she wasn't nearly as scary-looking as most last-stage AIDS patients I'd seen. Her face was intact; she was pale, but still pretty. Other than her hair, which had fallen out in handfuls and showed an inch of white at the root, nothing marked her as a woman who would be dead in six weeks.

When we settled on the sofa, Elsie, the nurse, brought us tea. "She so glad you here," she said, as if Carole weren't sitting next to me. "Arncha, Cal?"

"Huh?" Carole had drifted away.

"Glad? Arncha glad Mark come to be with you?"

"Oh." She looked at me, trying to fix me with her half-good eye, as if she'd forgotten I was there. "He's my best friend. We love each other, don't we?" she added, taking my hand.

"Very much." Her hand was cold. Blue veins showed through the skin.

"Yes." Carole kept hold of my hand but drifted away again, a gentle, peaceful look on her face. "It's so strange," she said, drifting back.

"What is?"

"Losing everything. You know, that's what I was scared of—losing. I always held on so hard. I was so scared I'd end up with nothing. But then, no matter how hard you fight, you end up with nothing anyway." Carole paused. "It's funny," she said.

"Really?"

"It's not what you thought it would be at all. The more you lose, the lighter you feel. It's really true. I've never been happier in my life. You don't know it till you get there. You can't. But now that I've got nothing left, He seems so close."

Carole touched the crucifix around her neck. "Honestly. I can feel Him right here with me, close to my heart. Right beside Mother Meera. They're both holding me."

She closed her eyes and a calm look came over her, half-smiling, like the da Vinci virgin I had hanging on my wall.

"She do this a lot," whispered Elsie. "She got the spirit, really, like nobody I seen before. She pray all the time. Especially when Virginia come."

"Hon-eee!" squealed Sister Virginia when she arrived the next afternoon and reached out to hug Carole. "You're looking good! Very good indeed, my honey."

Virginia was in her eighties, I guessed, and not your standard picture of a nun. She was thin as a bone and dressed from head to toe in purple—purple scarf over her blonde wig, purple pants suit, purple bangles, purple eyeglass frames, purple galoshes that she removed to reveal purple tennis shoes. "Sweet Jesus, what a day," she said of the rain. "Do I have goodies for you, my honey—good things to make you feel good." Virginia spoke to Carole like a child, and Carole responded accordingly, sitting on the edge of her bed, waiting for her presents. "What did you bring me?"

Virginia's eyes lit up. "Just wait!" She rummaged in her bag. "First of all, the secret of life!" She produced a bottle and held it close to Carole's eyes so that she could read it. "It's royal jelly, the elixir of the queen bee, and it's going to give you energy. I use it every day, and I swear to the Lord it's made me a different person."

Virginia spooned out a portion of the golden liquid and brought it to Carole's lips. "Isn't that delicious, honey?"

"Mmmm."

"Would you like some—I'm sorry, I didn't catch your name."

"Mark. Yes, please." She handed me the jar and a fresh spoon. "It really is good for everything. Have you ever seen how much energy bees have?"

Within minutes after Sister Virginia's arrival, the atmosphere of the apartment had changed completely, lifting the sickroom feeling. The royal jelly was doing its trick.

"Now wouldn't we like to pray?" Virginia asked.

The four of us, including Elsie, gathered around the bed. Virginia placed her hands on Carole's head, which hurt her constantly now because of the lesions. Virginia closed her eyes and I watched her as she began. "Sweet Jesus," she said as if talking to someone present, "help our child Carole to be well, Lord, help her to feel your love, and ease her poor head, sweet one, give her surcease from the pain. And dearest Mother, help in this healing.

"Hail Mary," she said, and we all joined in: "full of grace, the Lord is with thee . . ."

As Virginia stood over Carole, blessing her, I saw a glow appear around them. It was clear as the light coming from the bedside lamp, and aura surrounding their joined figures. I had the impression that a presence had descended on the room, sweet as the honey we'd just tasted, smoothing out the edges and drawing us together. With this presence came a silence that stopped Virginia's prayer and Elsie's fidgeting, until all you could hear for several minutes was the sound of our breathing.

When Virginia said, "Thank you, Mary," and made the sign of the cross over Carole, Carole opened her eyes and looked quite different. Her face was flushed and peaceful. She touched her head, confused.

"It doesn't hurt," she said. "You did it again, Virginia, it doesn't hurt."

"I didn't do it, honey. It's the blessing. Now, are you ready to receive the host?" Virginia took a beautiful gold case, ornately engraved with what appeared to be gemstones set on each of its four sides, from her pocket. Opening it, she removed a Communion wafer and held it in front of Carole's open mouth. "The body of Christ," she said, placing the white orb on Carole's tongue.

"And look what else I brought my baby," Virginia said.

"Doughnuts!" Carole squealed.

One sunny but blustery afternoon, Carole asked me to take her to the beach. There was no one on the sand for a mile in either direction, and we walked very slowly, Carole clutching my arm, careful to avoid rocks and driftwood, which were excruciating to her tender feet. It took us ten minutes to walk twenty yards, from the parking lot to the water's edge. We sat down on a tree trunk and looked out at Puget Sound and the islands in the distance.

Carole held my arm and we didn't talk. The loveliness of the view, the fragility of my friend leaning against me, the tacit suspicion we shared that this would be her last time at the ocean, was too upsetting for words. When I looked at Carole there were tears in her eyes, but they seemed to be tears of joy, not sadness. She'd reached that point at the end when every moment feels like a victory, a culmination. There was nowhere in the entire world that Carole would rather have been than sitting there on a log with me, looking out at the water.

At first, when the scent came, I hardly noticed it: a sweet wood smell like the air of India, like flowers on a barbecue. When I focused on it, however, the scent became more pronounced. I looked around for a bonfire, a campsite, something smoking. Carole was looking around as well. "Do you smell that?" she asked. "It's like incense."

Then I got it. The smell we'd both noticed at the same moment was exactly like the smell of the *darshan* room at Mother Meera's house. "Mother's incense," Carole whispered before I could say a word. Neither of us could understand it. The day was windy, there was no one on the beach for miles. This sweet smoke seemed to have come to us out of nowhere, a kind of message from Meera herself.

A few nights later, I made Carole her favorite dinner of meat loaf and mashed potatoes. She tried to muster enthusiasm for the meal, but when everything was laid out with candles, she excused herself to go to the bathroom.

"Are you all right?" I called out when she hadn't come back after ten minutes. Nothing. I opened the door and found her standing in the dark, bent over the sink, being sick. When I touched her shoulder, her body suddenly went rigid, her head snapped back and she started shaking, eyes rolling into their sockets as she gasped for air, then stopped breathing.

I held her tight in front of the mirror, staring with disbelief at the reflection: Carole stiff and covered with vomit; my face next to hers, hands around her belly, caught in a surreal tableau.

"Carole," I said. No response. I moved my hand across her open eyes. No response. This is it, I thought, she's going to die right here in my arms. I dragged her into the hallway and laid her out on the carpet, torn between calling 911 and letting her go. But I couldn't just leave her there, not knowing if she was in pain. I ran to the phone and called the medics. Within three minutes, five men were there.

Within the hour, the seizure passed and Carole returned to consciousness at the hospital. When she opened her eyes, she didn't know where she was, how she got there, or what had happened.

"Call the girls," she said. That night, Jamie and Marcy arrived and we gathered in Carole's room, along with Elsie and Sister Virginia. Carole was sitting up, with Jamie brushing her hair and Marcy trying to feed her oatmeal.

When the doctor came in, he asked Carole if she would like us to leave. She said no. He stood close to the bed while we looked on.

"If we continue to treat you," the doctor said, "it may be effective for a short time." Carole stared at him blankly. Jamie and Marcy looked scared.

"And if you don't?" she asked.

"You'll slip into a coma by the end of the day and go by the end of the weekend."

No one stirred. The doctor took her hand and squeezed it, checking her pulse. He said that he would leave her to make her own decision. Carole looked at me and I shook my head once.

"Stop the treatment," she said.

I made an altar in the room: a photograph of Carole smiling, the flowers my sister Belle had sent from California, candles, a picture of Mother Meera, a pigeon feather that blew in the window. Carole's eyes followed me from her pillow, but I couldn't tell if she could really see. When I spoke to her, she didn't answer, but when I held her hand, she squeezed back. Sister Virginia's boss, Father Dave, came and sang *Salve Regina* by the bed. Carole's eyes closed, fluttered open, and closed again for a long time. The nurse came in and disconnected the IV bags, leaving only the glucose to keep her hydrated. We waited.

At one point during the night, when Marcy and I were talking in low voices, Carole suddenly said, "Stop that whispering over there," scaring us to death. I sat on the bed and took her hand.

"Carole," I said loudly. "Can you hear me?" I shook her arm. "Are you awake?"

"Um," she murmured.

"Open your eyes," I said. She cracked them open. The pupils were dilated and unfocused. "Who am I?" I asked her.

"Mother Meera," she said.

I wanted it to be over, and so did the girls. It's embarrassing to see how impatience, then anger, then shame develop at a deathbed vigil. Even before the person you love has stopped breathing, you're already planning the funeral, planning your escape, planning your recovery.

I wondered about the words of enlightened masters regarding individual death. In the discourses of Meher Baba, I came across this passage: "A sane attitude toward death is possible only if life is considered impersonally and without any attachment to particular forms. . . . What the worldly individual craves is the continuation of his own form and other particular forms with which he is entangled." Here, as often happened, I felt myself split down the middle between enlightened wisdom and the pain of my own entangled heart. I could imagine the dispassion Meher Baba was describing, but something seemed to be missing as well, an appropriate cherishing of form, a reverence for what is human and small and specific.

There was a danger in spiritual posturing, pretending to be more detached than one was. Watching Carole die, I decided that I would rather be broken and messy and sad than pretend not to be grieving. Much as I wanted the sort of long view Meher Baba spoke of, I realized that I wanted it for many of the wrong reasons. Part of me aspired to liberation so as not to feel anymore; part of me still imagined that enlightenment would help me not be touched. In fact, this was completely untrue.

Once a disciple saw Mother Meera weeping on the stairs of her house. "What is it?" he asked her.

Mother pointed to her heart. "*Schmerz*," she said. Pain. As simply as that. Even for a saint like her, pain was there to be lived with.

When Mr. Reddy died, they say that Mother Meera was disconsolate. This was not a sign of her unenlightenment, but a proof of her divinity, which includes human frailty.

On the third day after Carole went into a coma, I left the hospital to meet a friend for dinner. Naturally, Carole waited until the hour I was gone to slip away. When I called from the restaurant, Jamie answered in hysterics.

"She just died," she said.

I was there in five minutes. I ran down the hall; the girls were outside the room with the doctor. I went inside and closed the door.

Carole's mouth and eyes were open. Her head was turned to the side, facing me. I wailed. I hadn't expected to. I had thought that I was prepared for this. But from the depths of me came a howl that felt like it was coming from somebody else. For a long time I charged around the room sobbing, burying my head in the blankets. I didn't know if I was weeping for myself or for my friend.

When my tears finally passed, I sat by the bed and looked into Carole's eyes. Then I closed mine and held her left wrist between my fingers. My mind was filled with a strange vision—an upsweep of rainbow-bodied birds flying together into blackness, a vision of extreme, living beauty. I followed them for a long time, observing their many-colored forms as they rose and dispersed. When I opened my eyes, I felt calm.

Without thinking, I found myself moving around the room, as if I were being guided. I laid a yellow daisy on Carole's breast, a purple Christmas cactus flower at her feet, and made the sign of the cross with holy water on her forehead and feet. I took the rosary she was clutching in her hand and dropped it into my pocket. After looking once more into her eyes, I closed them gently with my thumbs.

Two weeks later, with Carole's ashes in a can, I boarded a plane to Frankfurt.

PART FOUR

MAN THINKS, GOD LAUGHS

TWENTY-ONE

THALHEIM COULDN'T HAVE looked bleaker than on the day I arrived the third week of November 1991. The sky was iron gray, and a heavy rain was falling during the hour it took me to travel by train from the airport to Limburg station. I could hardly see the church spire at the center of the village from my taxi window as we pulled off the highway, and the driver slowly made his way through the fog, stopping finally in front of Mother Meera's house.

Setting my suitcase on the stoop, I remembered how I'd felt on the day when Alexander first brought me there, six years before—lost in my life, full of grief—and realized that here I was again, arriving on Mother Meera's doorstep with my heart in my hands.

"Hello, darling." Alexander opened the door.

"You came," I said. I'd called him in Paris after Carole died.

"Of course I came," he replied, opening his arms, dissolving whatever nervousness I'd had at seeing him again. "Now come give Granny a hug."

I laid my head on Alexander's shoulder, smelling the familiar mix of Guerlain and damp cashmere. We stood there for a long time in the doorway, hugging.

"You look like you've been through hell," he said.

"You don't know."

"But I do," he said. Alexander had met Carole; he knew the depth and complexity of our friendship. "You did the right thing by staying with her to the end," he said. "Now, something new can start."

"God, I hope so."

He took my suitcase and the shopping bag containing the can with Carole's ashes, and led me up the stairs. I'd been surprised, when I called Adilakshmi, to be invited to stay in Mother's house, since rooms were scarce and requests many. I was even more surprised to find that the room they had given me was directly under Mother's own quarters, with windows looking out over her private garden.

"The presidential suite," Alexander said, depositing my things. The house had retained the same otherworldly silence I remembered from my first visit, when my ears were filled with that weird ringing— now, the only sound I heard was shuffling overhead as Mother Meera walked across her room.

"Has she changed?" I asked.

"Mother?" Alexander asked. "Of course not."

That afternoon, we walked up into the woods behind the village. The rain had stopped, the roads were muddy, horses watched us from the fields. We passed the cemetery where Mr. Reddy was buried, and crossed up toward the forest, talking non-stop as always, catching up on each other's life. Alexander told me about his new book, the latest dramas of his nutty friends in Paris, his most recent, doomed love affair with a man who couldn't love him back.

"I thought you were cured of romance," I said. "I thought I'd stripped you of your last illusion."

"I'll never be cured," Alexander laughed. "What would life be without romance?"

"Calm?" I suggested.

"Calm is *not* my path. You should know that as well as anyone."

"At least you *know* what your path is," I answered. "Sometimes I feel more confused than when we met." At that moment, the sky opened up and a deluge poured down on us, sending us running for cover into one of the hunters' shelters that were scattered throughout the woods. We climbed the ladder into the four-by-four hut on stilts, bundled in, huddled next to each other on a bench as the storm thundered down around us.

I talked about my doubts and confusion, admitting to Alexander how after all these years of seeking, reading, doubting, analyzing— trying to understand my inner life—I still sensed that there was something missing. "It's like I'm always seeking but never finding," I said. "Always moving but never arriving."

"*Neti neti*," said Alexander, wringing out his muffler. "Not this, not that."

"Exactly."

"You're never satisfied. Something keeps you pushing further."

"Questions," I answered. "Always more questions."

Alexander smiled. "But don't you see that *is* your path? You're a doubting Thomas. You'll need to keep asking more and more questions until there's nothing left to ask."

"I'll probably be dead by then."

"That's what you said on our first date. Remember?"

How could I forget walking along the Hudson River and Alexander asking me point-blank what I believed were my chances of being alive in five years. Without hesitation, I'd answered, "Fifty-fifty."

"That was six years ago," he reminded me. "You've already beaten your own odds."

He had a point: not only that, but other than my exhaustion after nursing Carole, I'd never felt better in my life. Except for a drop in my T cells and the occasional swollen gland, I hadn't been sick a day from this virus. "It's hard to believe," I admitted.

"Be grateful."

"I am. But now I need some answers from you know who."

"Then you must ask."

"How?"

"Go up the stairs and knock on the door."

The thought of actually doing this sent a wave of terror through me. "I can't figure out why she scares me so much."

"It's the love," Alexander replied.

Was that it? Was I afraid of the love I'd sensed emanating from Mother Meera? Was I afraid that it would steal my power, force me to live another kind of life, if I surrendered? Was I afraid that although I was used to handling profanity, holy love of the kind I felt in Mother Meera's presence would finally sweep my defenses away and turn me into someone else?

Perhaps, but there were other fears as well. "What if she won't talk to me?"

"She will talk," said Alexander, "if you're sincere. But then," he added with a chuckle, "you may have to listen."

In the days that followed, I debated how best to approach Mother Meera, playing out scenarios in my mind, scrapping them, starting over, pacing my room like a trapped animal, while Alexander scribbled away in his room in the basement. I would sit listening to her move above my head, and have imaginary conversations with her; or I would talk to Carole, tucked away in her can in the black Barneys bag in the closet, asking her advice. The answer was always the same— *go upstairs*—but every time I left my room and stood at the bottom of the stairs, looking up at Mother Meera's closed door, I turned back.

When Friday rolled around, I dressed carefully for the first day of *darshan* and joined Alexander in the room. There were many more chairs now, and at six-thirty, the door opened and a hundred visitors filed in, greeted with a smile by Adilakshmi. Besides the Germans I recognized from my first visit, there were several plain-looking neighbors from the village, a few Indians, a dozen Americans, and an orthodox Jew wearing a yarmulke. The crowd took their seats and gradually, as the hour approached, stopped whispering and settled down as a silence descended on the room.

The church bells tolled seven in the village tower, and when the last chime ended, I heard the door open upstairs. Automatically, the crowd rose to its feet, all eyes on the door. Then Mother Meera was there—in a gold sari, her eyes lowered to the ground as she made her way through the aisle of people and settled on her chair. After a moment's pause, Adilakshmi knelt first on the carpet and put her head in Mother Meera's hands.

I'd imagined this moment a thousand times in the years since I'd first come here; I'd pictured myself in this room, trying to understand what had actually happened to my heart when I first saw her, and wondering if it would happen to me again. Now, for the next two hours, I sat watching *darshan* proceed like clockwork, Mother Meera unwavering. After kneeling in front of her myself, I stared into Mother Meera's strange eyes, searching for some kind of response to the questions buzzing through my mind. I saw nothing but sky.

A week passed, then two, then three; still, I didn't dare to climb the stairs. Once, leaving the house, I saw Mother Meera on the slanted roof thirty feet up in a parka and work boots, hammering shingles; she stared down at me, smiling intently. Mostly, she remained indoors, out of sight, mysterious.

The day of my proposed departure came and went, and when I requested permission to stay on in the house, I was told that I was welcome to remain for as long as I liked. Day after long monotonous day, when I wasn't watching Mother in *darshan*, I was holed up in my room writing, staring out the window at the dreary weather, walking for hours through the hills and forest and pastures. I had planned to come, lay Carole to rest, get some answers, and leave. But as the weeks passed, I was surprised to discover that, as much as I wanted to escape, I simply couldn't. Every time I resolved to go, to scatter Carole's ashes and leave without speaking to Mother, I heard a voice inside me say, as a kind of challenge: "You say you want to wake up, but do you really? Where are you going? There's nothing out there. Without deep roots, the plant cannot grow."

One day, when this refrain had frustrated me to the boiling point, I escaped into the woods and exploded.

"When are you going to help me?" I shouted. "When am I going to get some answers? I've had enough. It's time!" I stood there waiting for something to happen, watching the snow fall on the branches. Then, before I could change my mind, I ran down the path and into the village, up the stairs to Mother Meera's door.

"I'm sorry," I said when Adilakshmi answered. I was standing there dripping in wet clothes. "May I please talk to Mother Meera." Then I added. "Now?"

Adilakshmi looked down at my wet socks and smiled. "I will ask Mother," she said. When she closed the door, I could hear them speaking in low voices. After a minute, Adilakshmi returned. "Please come in," she said.

I walked across the threshold and followed Adilakshmi into the living room of Mother's apartment.

There was a fire in the hearth; the room was plain, pretty, with a view like mine over garden and fields. Mother Meera was sitting on a sofa, her hair disheveled, an old sweater over her sari, looking extremely young. When I sat down, she smiled.

"Hello, Mother," I said.

She continued smiling. Adilakshmi sat next to her and beamed.

For a moment, my mind went blank as it had done that first night on the stairs, when Alexander had introduced us. Now, Mother waited patiently for me to begin.

I started slowly, describing Carole's death, the experience we'd had smelling the incense together on the beach, the sense we'd shared that we were joined by fate. Mother listened and, when I was finished, inquired after my own health.

"I seem to be holding pretty steady," I said. There was another long pause, while Mother waited for me to continue. "I have so many questions," I told her.

"You may ask your questions," Adilakshmi chimed in. "You are welcome."

"Are you my master?" I blurted out, my voice nearly cracking.

Mother Meera smiled at me without saying a word, then glanced at Adilakshmi.

"Perhaps we should begin with another question," Adilakshmi gently suggested.

Feeling slightly embarrassed, uncertain as to whether I'd said the wrong thing, I approached from another direction. "I'm not sure if I believe in God," I said. "Why do I have so many doubts?"

"Doubt is good," Mother Meera replied. Her voice was deep, almost hoarse, strangely unsuited to her girlish appearance. "Doubt proves that you are sincere."

"But what about faith?" I asked.

Mother spoke a few words in her native Telugu to Adilakshmi, who translated. "Mother says that even atheists believe in something. You must find the thing that you love and begin there. This love is the way to the divine."

"I keep hoping that it will just *happen* one day," I admitted. "Suddenly my heart will open and I'll know that God is real."

Mother Meera shook her head. "First the mind must be opened," she said in halting English. "Then the heart."

"I thought it was the other way around."

"Without an open mind, the heart cannot hear," she added. "But first you must be calm and listen."

"Is that why you give *darshan* in silence?"

Mother Meera smiled. "Talk you can get anywhere," she said.

It was a tremendous relief to hear Mother speak, to finally have confirmation—in the spontaneous assurance with which she was responding to my questions—that she was indeed a wise being, that the mastery I'd sensed in her was not wishful thinking.

Now I continued. "There are so many gurus out there," I said. "It's hard to tell the difference between the real ones and the fakes. How can I know if a person is really enlightened or not?"

"By the joy in your heart when you are with them," she said simply.

"Is enlightenment rare?"

"Very."

"And can you actually help a person toward it?"

"Of course," Mother Meera said. "But first you must be ripe."

Adilakshmi chimed in. "Mother says that the soul of the seeker must be *pakka*, like a juicy fruit that falls from the tree!" she sang, delighted by her own metaphor.

"I see," I said. "And am I ripe?"

Mother Meera smiled but said nothing, instead looking away at the fire crackling in the hearth.

"All right, then, tell me *this*. Is struggle necessary, or do I wait for my soul to ripen?"

"You must try hard," Mother replied. "When there is no effort, there is no result. You cannot feel the joy of progressing."

"To feel that joy is why you are here," added Adilakshmi.

"But *am* I progressing? I'm really not sure sometimes."

Mother Meera nodded her head. "Yes," she said. "You are much stronger than when you first came."

With those words, a weight lifted from my heart. After all these years of doubting, judging my confusion and backslides, wondering why—when others chose paths and stuck to them—I was always so restless and discontented, to hear Mother Meera confirm that I had moved forward nonetheless eased my doubt and gave me the courage to ask again my most pressing question. "Does that mean that *you* are my master then?"

Adilakshmi glanced at Mother. After a long pause, Mother Meera looked me straight in the eye and said softly, "I am not your master. I am your mother."

What did she *mean?* "I'm sorry," I said. "I don't understand." I waited for her to elaborate, but just then, before I could press her further, my mind went blank. In fact, my thoughts seemed to disappear completely, replaced by a wave of peace and silence. For several minutes, I could do nothing but gaze absently at the flowers on the table. When, after several minutes, I came around, Mother Meera was smiling at me. I knew that our interview was over.

In the days that followed, I mulled over what she had said. What did Mother Meera *mean* by saying that she was my *mother*, not my master? I realized that Dr. Pushpa had been right: Mother Meera had indeed answered me with a riddle, but though I was frustrated not to receive a simple yes or no, I was deeply intrigued as well, sensing that behind this riddle lay the answer to a question even more profound than the one I had asked.

I talked this over with Alexander, who was atypically reticent. "Well?" I asked him on our daily walk. "What do you think she meant by *that*?"

"I could explain it, but I won't."

"Why not?"

"There are some things even I don't interfere with."

"The last thing I want is another mother," I whined. Images of Ida and the dark, loveless atmosphere of my childhood flashed across my mind.

"You may not want it, darling, but it may be what you need."

"Huh?"

But Alexander wouldn't talk.

Several days later, when I returned to the house, there was a message from Belle in California. "Call Mommy," she said when I dialed back.

"What's wrong?" I asked.

"Nothing. She just wants to talk to you."

This was unusual—my mother never wanted to just talk, especially when I was abroad. I waited an hour or so, preparing myself for what Ida might have to say, then dialed her number in Los Angeles.

Ida answered after one ring. I could tell when she said hello that she had been drinking. In recent years, vodka and orange juice had become her best friend.

"It's Mark, Mom."

"Mark?" she said, sounding bleary. "Where are you?"

"Germany."

"What are you doing *there*?"

"I have a friend."

My mother laughed. I had never ceased to amaze her; she could never understand how a son of hers had become a world traveler. "My wandering Jew."

"What's wrong?" I asked.

"You know what today is?"

February second. My thirty-fourth birthday was coming the following week. "It's not for another three days, Mom."

"Don't you remember?"

I scanned my mind for associations. Then it hit me: it had been three days before my birthday, in 1978, that my sister Marcia had committed suicide. Today was the anniversary of her death. "I'm sorry, Mom. I forgot."

I heard my mother cover the receiver. I hadn't heard her cry for years—I could recall clearly the few times my mother had wept when I was a boy, how I'd felt that my universe was coming apart. Now, hearing Ida's grief eight thousand miles away, I was seized by my old panic again—needing to save her, stop the sadness, keep her from sliding into darkness—and not being able to. I thought of what would happen to her if I got sick, how unbearable it would be to witness her pain, to live with the guilty feeling that, without meaning to, I'd dealt my mother the coup de grace.

"Mommy," I said, quietly. "Please don't cry."

"To lose a child," she whispered. "Tell me the truth. Are you okay?"

"I'm fine, Mom. Really."

"Don't think that because I don't ask it doesn't scare the hell out of me."

"I know that."

"Will you come home soon?" she asked. "I'm not gonna be around forever either."

"I will, Mom. Soon. I promise."

"And will you light a candle for your sister?"

It was our tradition to light a *Yahrzheit* candle every year on the anniversary of a death. "I will."

"Promise me," my mother said.

"I promise."

"If you don't," she said, "I'll feel it."

Behind the monotonous backdrop of Thalheim during those weeks, strange things began to happen, as they had during my first visit. Most mornings, I would awaken with vivid recollection of highly symbolic dreams containing obvious messages, almost as if I had been given some subconscious instruction in my sleep. Sometimes these night visions were so intense that the boundary between sleep and waking seemed nearly indistinguishable. I was thinking while asleep, dreaming while awake, these states blurring and bleeding into each other. On numerous occasions, sitting at my desk, I would fall into a spontaneous trance; first, my eyes would get heavy, and a warm sensation would fill me, as if descending from the top of my head, paralyzing my body. With my eyes closed, my mind darting around for explanations, I would observe myself from the outside, sitting there stuck, like a bug in amber. These unexpected interludes lasted for as long as an hour. When they passed, I was relaxed, and filled with wonder.

Once, when I was typing at the computer, I felt this golden warmth come over me and heard an inner voice say, "Stop." I ignored, the voice and kept on typing. "Stop," it said again. Once more, I continued with my work until, a minute later, my computer froze. I pressed the keys of my perfectly functional machine and nothing happened—no letters appeared on the screen. Not until the next day did the keyboard begin to work again, as mysteriously as it had stopped.

On February 10, sitting at my desk as usual, I felt an experience beginning. Knowing better than to fight it, I put down my pencil and waited. I felt the familiar warmth flow from the top of my head to my feet, immobilizing my body while my mind remained alert.

Then an unexpected thing happened. Inwardly, I saw the door to my room open and Mother Meera enter, as clearly as if she were actually there. She walked toward me, coming to within an inch of my face, then bent forward and leaned her forehead against mine. When the red dot painted between her eyebrows touched the same spot on me, I fell even more deeply into this rapture, tumbling for a long time into a well of tremendous sweetness, until I heard Mother's gravelly voice say, "Remember that I love you." Then she pulled her head away.

In that instant, the trance flipped into a nightmare, smothering me in a series of the most horrific images, which flashed in front of my eyes in 3-D, one after another in breakneck succession. There was my mother staring down at me from the open bathroom door, blood streaming down her neck; there was Joyce, fat and sobbing, holding her cold, blue baby; there was Belle in her hospital bed, extending the twisted fingers of her hand in my direction; there was Marcia, dangling her legs off the roof of a building, staring down, knowing she was going to die; there she was in the ICU, her lips shaking as the medics beat her back to life; and shooting through these vivid, awful memories, the icy, solitary terror I'd felt as a child, helpless to prevent this violence. On and on the experience went, one ugly image piling into the next, a horror show of my own psyche.

Then as fast as it had started the nightmare was over. When I opened my eyes, I was on the floor, the left side of my body numb from head to toe. I lay there, sobbing, holding my belly, as I had as a child on the bathroom floor. Now, though I could feel this pain, I heard a voice repeating as well, "Remember that I love you."

This calmed me, and once I was still enough to listen, this subtle voice explained what had just happened. "As long as you believe that *this* is what being a child means," it seemed to say, "you can never feel at home in the world. You can never allow yourself to surrender. You can never love God."

This is what had been blocking me, I saw—something so obvious I had missed it. Before I was old enough to realize what was happening, childhood and everything it stood for had been fused with terror. I had decided *never* to be a child again, never to be innocent, believing that if I did, I would be destroyed. Now, lying on the floor of Mother Meera's house, I saw with crystal clarity that as long as I was terrified to be like a child, the orphan in my soul would never be at peace. I would never be able to love.

I ran downstairs and cried in Alexander's arms, much as I had done when I woke up that first morning in this house, feeling the wound in me beginning to open. Now I cried again, with even greater gratitude, knowing that that wound had begun to heal.

"I am your mother," Meera had told me, and now, with my fear of childhood exposed, I could begin to grasp the truth of what she meant. Just as Mother was not my master, but an embodiment of all-embracing love, so, she seemed to be saying, were all things in life facet of this great diamond. The Mother of creation had been speaking to me through everyone I'd ever encountered, in ten thousand voices and ten thousand ways: through the lesion on John's foot; through Bob and Alexander; through the S&M boy on Christopher Street; through Ariel Jordan; through Andy Warhol and Doris and the voices on my tape recorder, each with its own wisdom, its lesson, its message of how to live or how *not* to live; through Stephen Levine, Dr. Pushpa, and those dying in hospice; through Carole, of course, her love and her death; through the lives of saints, the dharma filtering through the world and into my heart; and finally through Ida— my own dark mother—broken as she had been by her grief. Through all these myriad voices, the Mother had been instructing me, never stopping for a minute.

This reminded me of a parable in which the enlightened seeker is compared to an infant sobbing in its mother's lap. The woman strokes her baby's head, rocks him against her breast with infinite love and infinite patience. Finally, when he can cry no more, the child begins to quiet down and, wiping his eyes, looks up to see the luminous face of the One who's holding him. He feels the softness of her belly and knows, for the first time, who and what he has always been, the progeny of this great mother, joined to her in body and spirit, never abandoned and never alone. When the baby finally sees her, the mother smiles, and seeing her grin, the child learns to smile too.

There was no master, I saw now, no one to take the burden or joys of life from me. There was only a mother to redirect me back to myself, and the light of understanding in my own heart. Just as a mother might prepare her child to move out into the world, Mother Meera was reminding me to stop looking outside myself for answers; to be still and listen to the voice of my own soul, trusting that I was in good hands. My own life, after all, was the only path I needed.

*

That evening, during *darshan*, I watched Mother Meera, hour after hour, taking head after head into her hands. I began to think sadly about Ida, stuck in her depression, struggling through her life-long pain. Just then, an old blind woman, shabbily dressed, rose from her chair and was helped by Adilakshmi to the carpet in front of Mother. When Meera touched her face, I saw the pain drain out of the blind woman's features. I closed my eyes and pictured Ida kneeling there, being blessed for the first time. I imagined the sadness melting from her as my mother had a moment's peace, a glimpse of faith, a touch of grace before she died. When I felt Meera's hands on my own head that evening, I imagined Ida at my side, taking the blessing with me.

I packed my bags the next morning—nearly three months to the day since I had arrived—and climbed the stairs to Mother Meera's door. When I knocked, she opened it herself.

"I think I understand what you meant now, Mother."

She stood there smiling. Her eyes were extremely bright. She nodded without saying a word.

"Please bless Carole," I said. "And my mother."

"Yes," she said in her low voice.

"May I come back and stay with you again?" I asked. Mother Meera looked at me. "The door is always open," she said.

Alexander and I set out toward the cemetery with Carole's ashes. We found a spot at the back of the graveyard, close to a tall wooden Christ hanging from a cross, and cleared a patch of ground beneath a berry bush.

Carefully, I pried open the lid of the can containing Carole's remains. Could this really be all that was left of my friend, I asked myself, looking at the pint of dust. Her love, her belongings, her questions, her infectious laughter, could all that be gone except for this? It seemed impossible.

"It's like a dream," I said to Alexander.

I carefully poured the fine white powder on the ground. I smoothed out the pile with a leaf, then stuck it in the middle of the mound like a tiny flag. From my pocket, I took the rosary that Carole had been holding when she died, and placed it next to a stick of incense. "Hail Mary, full of grace, " we said, watching the smoke and ash as we recited the prayer that Carole had loved so much.

When we'd finished, Alexander kissed me on either cheek, then quietly slipped out of the graveyard. I watched him go—this extraordinary man, shoulders hunched against the cold—and felt a wave of love for him beyond my ability to express.

I sat with Carole for another hour, then set off up the road toward the forest, past the beer hall and the grocery store, across to the west path that led to the darkest part of the woods. Something was over, I knew: I'd finally turned the corner I'd been balking at for all these years. Walking along the road in that moment all cynicism had left me. I knew that the miracle, the incomprehensible blessing of life itself, was as real as the muddy ground beneath my shoes. The air and sun and trees were divine, the entire world charged with an immortal essence. I'd known this once when I was a boy but accidentally lost that wonder. Now, as Mother Meera had confirmed, the door was open again, and with that opening, words I had never quite believed—God, divinity, miracles—lost their power to block my way.

These words had held me hostage to doubt—now I threw them

away. No more *divine*, no more *God*, no more *spirit*, no more *other*, I thought; only this, here, now, in all its splendid, factual nature, including those worlds I could not see. What could all this be *but* divine? I asked myself. What could I have imagined this earth to be but a wholly splendid miracle? I saw how deluded I'd been not to see what was right in front of my eyes: that all things in creation were holy, even the ugly, violent, and incomprehensible. What had once appeared to me as a loose jumble of separate things now seemed to come together as one presence. I thought of Pushpa's metaphor of the goldsmith hammering ore into many shapes—pine tree, horse, mountain, me—but all of them fashioned from the same substance. I'd denied the smith—half the world was denying it—but how amazingly foolish this was! The world was made lucid, cohesive, alive, by the very thing we questioned most. We had been set up to make a false choice—between our minds and our mystery. What a relief it was to realize now that they were the same thing.

I thought this as I circled back down the road, over the bridge, past the cemetery where Carole was and where, I believed, I would be when my time came. I stopped at the gate and looked inside at the tombstones, imagining the many lives and stories that were buried there. I breathed deeply, easily—the fist between my ribs was gone for good. I wasn't scared; I wasn't sad; the line between me and those bodies underground was sacred and unbroken. We were separate now only by degrees, as shade from quiet light. I was here, they were here—incontestably as *it* was.

I walked from the graveyard toward the field, where horses were huddled against the cold, their winter-fur heads resting together. The dead were behind me; ahead, spaciousness and light, ground to be traveled, heartaches, bliss. I turned and made my way back toward the village.

ACKNOWLEDGMENTS

The author wishes to thank the following people for their indispens-
able help with the book: Susan Peterson Kennedy, Barbara Graham,
Joy Harris, Eve Ensler, Deborah Treisman, Mary South, Paula Allen,
Robert Levithan, James Lecesne, Florence Falk, Louis Morhaim,
Katharina Tapp, Andrew Harvey, Paul Bellman, M.D., and Mother
Meera, whose extraordinary presence inspired this journey.

ABOUT THE AUTHOR

Mark Matousek is the award-winning author of seven books, including the memoirs *The Boy He Left Behind* and *When You're Falling, Dive.* His writing has appeared in many publications, including *The New Yorker, O: The Oprah Magazine, Details, Tricycle, Good Housekeeping, Harper's Bazaar,* and *The Village Voice,*

Photo by Karen Fuchs

as well as anthologies such as *Wrestling with the Angel, Voices of the Millennium, Oprah's Best Life,* and *A Memory, a Monologue, a Rant and a Prayer.* He blogs for *Psychology Today* and offers courses in creativity and spiritual growth around the world using the Writing to Awaken method.

Born in Los Angeles, Matousek graduated from the University of California, Berkeley; won a fellowship to study at Worcester College, Oxford; and earned an M.A. in English Literature from UCLA. In 1981, he moved to New York, working for Reuters International and *Newsweek* before becoming the first staff writer and senior editor for Andy Warhol's *Interview* magazine, interviewing hundreds of famous figures.

After leaving publishing in 1985, Matousek spent a decade as a freelance writer and dharma bum in Europe, India, and the United States. For *Common Boundary*, he wrote a column, "The Naked Eye," and the National Magazine Award-nominated exposé "America's Darkest Secret." He co-edited Ram Dass's *Still Here*, worked with Sogyal Rimpoche on *The Tibetan Book of Living and Dying*, and collaborated with Andrew Harvey on the book and documentary *Dialogues with a Modern Mystic*. Matousek founded The Seekers Forum, a global online community for nonsectarian spiritual dialogue, and co-founded V-Men, the male arm of V-Day, Eve Ensler's movement to end violence against women and girls. A faculty member at the New York Open Center; the Omega Institute; 1440; Esalen; the Rowe Center; Hollyhock; and Omega Blue Spirit, Costa Rica; he lives with his partner, David Moore, in Springs, New York.

Printed in the USA
CPSIA information can be obtained
at www.ICGtesting.com
JSHW082156140824
68134JS00014B/269